The CORPORATE FORMS *Kit*

Ted Nicholas

UPSTART
a division of Dearborn Publishing Group, Inc.

While a great deal of care has been taken to provide accurate and current information, the ideas, suggestions, general principles and conclusions presented in this book are subject to local, state and federal laws and regulations, court cases and any revisions of same. The reader is thus urged to consult legal counsel regarding any points of law—this publication should not be used as a substitute for competent legal advice.

© 1980, 1982, 1983, 1984, 1985, 1986, 1987, 1988, 1989, 1991, 1992, 1995 by Ted Nicholas

Published by Upstart Publishing Company, Inc.
a division of Dearborn Publishing Group, Inc.

Printed in the United States of America

95 96 97 10 9 8 7 6 5 4 3 2 1

Library of Congress Cataloging-in-Publication Data

Nicholas, Ted, 1934–
    The corporate forms kit / by Ted Nicholas.
      p.   cm.
    Includes index.
    ISBN 0-936894-91-1 (alk. paper)
    1. Coorporation law—United States—Forms. I. Title.
KF1411.N498 1995
346.73′066′0269—dc20
[347.306660269]   95-13921
                                            CIP

Books by Ted Nicholas

The Corporate Forms Kit

The Business Agreements Kit

The Complete Guide to Consulting Success (coauthor, Howard Shenson)

The Complete Guide to Nonprofit Corporations

The Complete Guide to "S" Corporations

The Executive's Business Letter Book

43 Proven Ways To Raise Capital for Your Small Business

The Golden Mailbox: How To Get Rich Direct Marketing Your Product

How To Form Your Own Corporation Without a Lawyer for under $75

How To Get a Top Job in Tough Times (coauthor, Bethany Waller)

How To Get Your Own Trademark

How To Publish a Book and Sell a Million Copies

Secrets of Entrepreneurial Leadership: Building Top Performance Through Trust and Teamwork

Contents

Chapter 3   Changes in Governance of Corporation   37

Forms

Chapter 4   Major Business Actions   57

Forms

Chapter 5   Dividends   95

Forms

Chapter 6   Compensation   107

Forms

Introduction

This book/disk package has been carefully designed to simplify the procedures involved in running a small or medium-sized company as a formal legal entity. It contains all the essential building blocks of a comprehensive system for recording corporation actions, yet it can be adapted to meet the special circumstances of almost any corporation.

Operating an enterprise through a corporate structure offers many advantages to the entrepreneur in a one-person operation. All of these advantages can be jeopardized, however, if you run the business as if the corporation did not exist. If you do not acknowledge your corporation, others won't either! In this way, you will supply them with ammunition to attack your personal assets—the company's debts and obligations will become yours. And the company's default or failure can wipe you out financially.

None of this has to happen, and you can help prevent it simply by taking the time to make sure that what you do in your business is done by and on behalf of your corporation. The best way to limit your own liability is to keep an ongoing record showing that your actions have been duly authorized and approved as actions of the corporation. To keep your corporation alive, you have to show that it is functioning as a legal entity in accordance with current corporate practices and the laws governing the official business of the corporation.

You can use the forms and resolutions in this new book/disk set to keep your corporation alive. The helpful instructions tell which forms to use to take the action you want, as well as how, and when, to use them. Each form has been carefully drawn up so that you can use it with little or no change in the wording and be sure of achieving the results you want.

Note: All forms on the following pages are complete and ready for your use on the enclosed IBM-compatible DOS disk. They can be used as is. New forms based on those in this book, with changes or modifications, can also be prepared.

Most of the forms are to be kept with inter-corporate records, usually a "corporate kit." (A loose-leaf book will suffice.) A few of the forms are to be filed with state agencies and are so indicated.

CHAPTER 1

How To Use This Kit

The Importance of Keeping Corporate Records

Time spent keeping business records is unproductive time. No business person has ever gotten rich because he or she kept tidy records. If corporation records can't help turn a profit, aren't they just a waste of time?

The answer is quite simple:

- Are you prepared to stand personally liable for all of the debts of the corporation that you assumed would be its debts and not yours?
- Are you prepared to sacrifice tax benefits you planned upon receiving when you formed your corporation?

Corporations keep records for different purposes. Big companies with billions at stake spend millions on records that thousands of shareholders, customers, employees, bureaucrats, suppliers and others may want to see to make sure that the company hasn't done something wrong.

Shareholders of smaller corporations, on the other hand, are less concerned with recordkeeping as a source for other businesspeople than they are with the need to demonstrate that the corporation is a real, functioning entity that is responsible for its debts.

In those instances, and they are far from rare, where the individual loses planned-for tax benefits or is held liable for the corporation's debts, it is never the fault of the "corporation." Rather, the blame lies with corporate personnel, officers, directors and shareholders who do not maintain books and records proving that the corporation had an existence separate and apart from its investors.

Courts have repeatedly and frequently imposed liability for a corporation's debts on its principals, i.e., its directors, officers and/or shareholders. In these cases, the courts can use either of two doctrines:

1. the alter ego doctrine, under which they hold that the corporation is no more than the alter ego of its shareholders, and, as such, its liabilities should be their liabilities; or
2. the piercing-the-corporate-veil doctrine, under which the courts rule that the corporation is really a sham and that it would be perpetrating a fraud to recognize its existence as a separate entity. Under this doctrine, the courts look through the corporate "veil" to its shareholders and hold them liable for the company's debts.

There is a common pattern to the fact in all of these cases: records were not kept at either the director or shareholder level. This means that if a payment gives the false appearance of being made for the benefit of a shareholder rather than the corporation, there is no documentation that the payment was, in fact, made for a corporate purpose.

Example 1: Assume that John and Fred are the only shareholders of a corporation, and that John does all of its outside sales work. Assume also that John uses his own car on which he makes monthly payments of $300. It becomes clear that John's bills for the use of his car will average out to $500 a month. John agrees with Fred that if the corporation will make the $300 monthly payment on the car, he will accept that in lieu of mileage, a savings to the corporation of at least $200 per month. Fred agrees and the payments are made for two years.

Now assume that Fred dies. Shortly thereafter, due to changed business conditions, the business fails, and has debts that are $20,000 more than its assets. Creditors sue John personally, pointing to the monthly car payments as a basis for piercing the corporate veil. If John and Fred had held a board meeting at which they passed a resolution and included the resolution in the minutes, the true corporate purpose of the payment would be clear. In the absence of such records, all John can do is provide his own self-serving declarations, which probably will not carry much weight in court.

In this example, as in so many other real-life cases, the downfall of the entrepreneur is that he or she can't prove that whatever was done, was done on behalf of the corporation and not for personal reasons. The very fact that the entrepreneur didn't keep records shows that he or she didn't respect the corporation's separate identity. And it hits where it hurts most—in his or her pocketbook as well as in the corporation's cash drawer.

Using *The Corporate Forms Kit*

The purpose of this kit is to ensure that if you treat your corporation as a separate entity, e.g., treat its assets as its own and not as your personal assets, you will not lose the advantages you sought when you formed the enterprise. The sections that follow put at your disposal a comprehensive yet easy-to-follow system for compiling a record of your corporation's actions. Corporations live only on paper, and *The Corporate Forms Kit* provides you with the papers a corporation needs to stay alive and functioning properly. **Note:** To ensure that the forms can be universally applicable, a blank line has been supplied at the top of these forms; to use the forms, you need only type the name of your corporation immediately above the line.

What does it take to keep a corporation alive? First, you must realize that a corporation consists of three groups of individuals: officers (managers) and employees, just as in any unincorporated business; a board of directors; and the shareholders. Of course, it is possible for one person to wear all three hats, as in a one-person corporation, but that just makes it more difficult—and more important—to establish and maintain a separate identity as the person switches from one role to another. The basic point is that two of these groups, the directors and the shareholders, exist only in corporations. Their existence and actions differentiate the corporation from other forms of business.

What do shareholders and directors do? The shareholders own the corporation, and this gives them the right to elect the directors and to approve or reject extraordinary corporate actions. These actions might include a merger or a liquidation. Individually, the shareholders are practically powerless, because they are only entitled to exercise these rights as a group. This means they have to get together in a meeting and vote "yes" or "no" on a particular proposal. Technically, this is the extent of the shareholders' role in the corporation. They can hold meetings and vote to approve board proposals. Technically, the shareholders can't, in themselves, carry out a resolution unless they also happen to be the corporation's directors or officers. But they are then acting as directors or officers and not as shareholders.

If the shareholders can only hold meetings and pass resolutions, it follows that records of meetings and resolutions will help prove that the corporation is being run as a legitimate separate entity. The same is true of the board of directors. The directors are essentially the elected representatives of the shareholders, and it is their job to watch over the corporation between meetings of shareholders. The directors report to the shareholders on what the company has done since the last meeting. Thus, the board of directors can do no more than the shareholders. They can hold meetings and pass resolutions. The biggest difference, perhaps, is that the board will probably hold more meetings and pass more resolutions than will the shareholders.

Written records of meetings and resolutions, especially in a format that meets legal standards for documentary evidence, can supply the proof you need that your corporation is alive and functioning as a separate legal entity.

The forms in this kit provide you with the basic building blocks of corporate life. By using these forms, you can create a corporate biography with records showing when, where and what events have occurred in the corporation's life. The corporation lives and speaks through its records; the forms in this kit comprise a system for documenting the events in the life of your corporation.

Forms for nearly a hundred different corporate actions are included in *The Corporate Forms Kit*. They have been carefully selected from thousands of resolutions, certificates, agreements and so on. Included here are the most commonly needed forms, written in the language that is most likely to give you the results you want. Generally, all you have to do is fill in the blanks with information that pertains to your corporation. Occasionally, however, you may wish to change the wording of a form to suit your particular situation. In every case, you should make sure that the language of the form is right for you. In some cases, you may find it necessary to consult a professional, such as an attorney or an accountant, to decide exactly what the form should say. Because the publisher cannot guarantee that the forms will fit your situations, it cannot assume any responsibility for their use. The forms in this book are designed to simplify your job of documenting your corporation's existence. They are not a substitute for your responsibility in deciding how you should document the actions of your corporation.

The Three Tiers of Corporate Management

In order to understand the significance of corporate documentation, you should understand the mechanics of how a corporation works. A corporation consists of three groups, or tiers, of management. The base tier consists of its shareholders, i.e., its owners. Shareholders do not play an activist role in corporate operations. In fact, they have but three major powers:

1. The right to elect directors

2. The right to approve or reject major corporate actions proposed by the board of directors, e.g., an amendment of the corporate charter or a proposed merger
3. The right to inspect corporate books and records

A shareholder, or even all shareholders acting in unison, does not have the authority or power to act in the corporation's name. A shareholder, for example, does not have the authority to bind the corporation to a contract for the purchase of a pencil. Under the law, shareholders "control" the corporation by electing directors to manage the business and affairs of the enterprise. Directors, in turn, bear the responsibility for setting corporate policies, financial and otherwise, and for overseeing those who run the business on a day-to-day basis, i.e., the officers of the corporation.

An individual director's powers are not really different from those of the individual shareholder. A director, acting as such, does not have the authority to represent the corporation in any contractual dealings, regardless of how insignificant the contracts may be. As a board, however, the directors do have the authority to bind the corporation in contractual dealings. They may delegate the power to officers, but if they do, the officer can act only within the parameters set by the board. If he or she does not, the officer can be held personally liable on the contract.

In most corporations, the board, in fact, does appoint officers, e.g., a president, vice president, secretary and treasurer. Officers run the day-to-day operations of the corporation, subject to the oversight of the directors. (In a one-person corporation, the sole shareholder may also serve as the corporation's sole director and officer; nevertheless, the procedures spelled out throughout this book should be followed by that individual just as if the corporation had several shareholders.)

With respect to officers, one warning should be noted. On occasion a corporation will appoint a figurehead as its president. So, for example, a local athlete may be named as the president of a bowling emporium and may appear there on a regular basis. The athlete may be only a figurehead whose real purpose is to draw customers to the business. He or she may not own any stock in the business or have any substantive authority to act for the corporation. In such cases, it is important that at least two documents note that the "president" has no authority to bind the corporation in any business matter: the board resolution that appoints the individual and the agreement between the individual and the corporation. Many courts tend to rule that the "president" of a corporation has the inherent power to act for the business and that people who deal with a corporation's president may safely rely on his or her power to bind the corporation in a contract. If, however, your board resolution and the president's contract with the corporation flatly deny the president the power to bind the corporation, and you immediately reject any contract he or she purportedly entered into on the corporation's behalf, you will have overcome any presumptions the court might otherwise be willing to make about the president's power to bind the corporation.

The authority of all officers should be spelled out in the corporation's bylaws, the board resolution appointing each officer and any employment agreement between the company and the officer. Traditionally, the courts view officers as having various ranges of authority. The broadest form of authority is possessed by the corporation's general manager, who generally is deemed to have authority to bind the corporation in any ordinary business matter. More often than not, a corporation's president is its general manager, but if your company assigns the specific title of *general manager* to a person, that individual will be viewed as having the authority to bind the company in ordinary matters.

Vice presidents usually are not viewed as having any authority to represent the corporation by virtue of their titles. There is one notable exception: if an individual is named vice president of a specific department, e.g., vice president of sales, then that person ordinarily will be viewed as having authority to bind the corporation to ordinary matters involving that department. So, for example, a vice president of sales would ordinarily be viewed as having the authority to hire an employee for the sales department. Similarly, a district or regional manager can be viewed as having authority to represent the district or regional office in ordinary business matters. If your company has such an employee, it is imperative that you follow the guidelines set out above for figurehead presidents if you intend to limit the authority of the vice president of a department or a district or regional sales manager.

Corporate secretaries and treasurers ordinarily are not viewed as having authority that ranges beyond the operations of their office, i.e., recordkeeping and financial administration.

In a real sense, the three tiers of individuals can be described as follows: the shareholders are the body of the corporation, the directors are the body's brain and the officers are its arms, legs, eyes and ears.

Just as every rule has its exception, so do the general rules described above. A number of states, including Delaware, provide that a corporation may be managed by its shareholders: they can act in lieu of a board or officers. Although this does make the operation of the corporation somewhat easier for one- or two-person businesses, i.e., where the same persons serve as the corporation's only shareholders, officers and directors, this option does not reduce in any meaningful manner the obligation to keep records. The shareholders of such corporations take on the duties, responsibilities and liabilities of directors. This, then, means that they must be able to support their actions in exactly the same way that directors and officers must support theirs. From a recordkeeping point of view, the same documents must be supplied. In practice, this means that the following rules apply:

1. If an action can be taken by the board alone, the documents must not reflect shareholder action.
2. If an action must be taken by both the board and shareholders, then only documents showing shareholder action must be prepared.

How Corporate Actions Are Accomplished

Five types of corporate actions must be addressed:

1. The election of directors
2. The appointment of officers
3. The setting of corporate policies
4. Ordinary business activities, e.g., purchases of ordinary goods, hiring of nonmanagerial employees
5. Extraordinary activities, e.g., hiring managerial employees, embarking on a proposed merger or changing the corporation's articles of incorporation

Each of these five actions requires at least one meeting and documentation; some require at least two meetings. Directors, for example, must be elected annually by shareholders. The election takes place at the annual shareholders' meeting. The meeting, in turn, requires written notice, and minutes must be taken of its proceedings.

Officers must be appointed by the board at a properly held board meeting. Again, there must be notice of the meeting, and minutes of the meeting must be taken. The same procedure must be followed by the board when it sets or changes corporate policy. Ordinary business activities of the corporation are carried out by the corporation's officers in conformity with the guidelines set out in board meetings. Those guidelines must be made known to officers.

Extraordinary matters require two meetings. First, there must be a meeting of the board at which the board decides to embark on the extraordinary matter. It does this by passing a resolution. (All board actions are authorized by a resolution, regardless of whether they are ordinary or extraordinary matters.) The shareholders must then be asked to vote on the extraordinary matter proposed by the board's resolution. Again, a shareholders' meeting, which may be the regular meeting or a special meeting called to consider the extraordinary matter, must be called by giving appropriate notice, and minutes of the meeting must be kept.

In Example 1, we noted how careless documentation could cause exposure to personal liability to outsiders. We also noted that the IRS can pierce the veil of an improperly run corporation and deny it the tax benefits for which it was formed. Another big risk run by the carelessly operated corporation is the unexpected liability flowing from one owner to another. Let's look at the following scenario:

Example 2: The board of directors of X Corporation consists of its three shareholders, Joe, Mary and Fred. At a board meeting, Joe, X's president, advises the board that their ten-year-old delivery van is on its last leg and that a replacement is needed. Mary and Fred agree, but point out that the corporation has been having cash flow problems. After discussion, the three agree that the corporation should not spend more than $20,000 on a new van and adopt a resolution that "Authorizes the president, Joe, to purchase the best van available at a price under $20,000."

Joe, however, succumbs to a hard-selling dealer from whom he has purchased several corporate vans in the past. He is talked into ordering a specially equipped van for $27,000. Assume that the board kept accurate minutes of the board meeting and that a copy of the resolution was given to Joe.

If the corporation is bound to complete the purchase, and it may well be obligated to do so, Joe can be held liable to X Corporation for exceeding his authority. Since the board kept minutes of the meeting at which the members decided to purchase the van, and the minutes of that meeting show that they clearly told him not to spend more than $20,000, Joe can be held liable to X Corporation for $7,000, since he exceeded his authority.

If the board had not kept minutes and had no written documentation, it would be the word of Mary and Fred against Joe (who, no doubt, would deny that he was given a $20,000 limit). A court, troubled by the lack of minutes, would probably rule that there was insufficient evidence to prove the claim against Joe.

This example should prove more than the fact that recordkeeping helped to avoid unintended liability. In reality, if a written resolution existed, Joe probably would not have purchased a $27,000 van. An added benefit of accurate recordkeeping, therefore, is that it ensures parties will do what they are supposed to do, thereby avoiding the kinds of misunderstandings among owners that often spell the death of a promising business.

The Record of Shareholders' Meetings—The Book of Minutes

As individuals, shareholders are powerless. They can act officially only as a group. This means that they have to get together in a formal meeting before they can legally bind the corporation. There are some exceptions where the shareholders can consent in writing to a particular action without having to hold a meeting. These instances are rare, and they are usually listed in the articles of incorporation.

Certain rules and procedures have to be followed for a gathering of shareholders to qualify as an official shareholders' meeting.

1. Every shareholder has to be given proper written notice of the date, time and place of the meeting, who is calling the meeting and an agenda of matters that will be considered at the meeting. Virtually every state requires a shareholder to have at least ten days' written notice of a meeting. Some states, notably Delaware, require that shareholders be given no more than 60 days' notice; others set the maximum notice at 50 days.

   Notice requirements can be effectively sidestepped in smaller corporations if each shareholder is willing to sign a waiver of notice at the shareholders' meeting. The waiver is then attached to the minutes of the meeting.

   Unscheduled or special meetings of shareholders also require written notice, although a signed waiver of notice can also be used at these meetings. For an unscheduled meeting to be legally convened, it is essential that the records show that proper notice was given, or that the shareholders signed a waiver of notice requirement. Further, the notice of a special meeting must contain a statement of the meeting's purpose.

   Your articles of incorporation or bylaws will specify where and when a shareholders' meeting can legally be held, and the book of minutes should show the date, time and place of each meeting. In this way, you can prove that the meeting complies with the legal requirements.

2. No business can be transacted at a shareholders' meeting unless a quorum is present. Therefore, it is essential that the book of minutes show that a quorum of shareholders attended the meeting. The articles of incorporation or the bylaws will usually state the size of the quorum, in terms of either the number of shareholders or the number of shares that must be represented at the meeting. For example, a bylaw that "two-thirds of all shareholders shall constitute a quorum" applies to the number of shareholders and not to the number of shares they own. On the other hand, a bylaw that "a majority of the outstanding stock shall constitute a quorum" means that a certain number of shares of stock must be represented, regardless of whether the stock is owned by one person or by thousands of people. If there is no rule on a quorum, every state corporation law states that a majority of the outstanding shares entitled to vote constitutes a quorum. Under such statutes, treasury and preferred stock, for example, would not be entitled to vote and would not be counted in determining whether a quorum is present.

3. Every shareholders' meeting must be presided over by a chairperson. It must also have a secretary to record what happened at the meeting. The bylaws will ordinarily designate these officials, such as by specifying that the president serve as chairperson and the secretary act as secretary. The minutes of each meeting should state who presided at the meeting and who acted as secretary.

4. One of the first items of business at every shareholders' meeting is to read and approve the minutes of the previous meeting. Once the minutes are approved, they become the best evidence of what occurred at the previous meeting. They are the most nearly conclusive proof of what the corporation is authorized to do. That is why it is important to show that the minutes have been read and approved as accurate.

5. Parliamentary procedure governs the conduct of meetings. This means that each matter to be acted upon has to be properly introduced by a motion from a member of the group and seconded by another member of the group. Then, every voting member of the group has to be given a chance to vote on the proposal. A sufficient number of votes, usually a majority of the quorum, must be cast in favor of the proposal for it to become binding on the corporation.

   It is not generally necessary to identify the person making or seconding a motion, nor is it essential to record the exact tally of votes, as long as the outcome is clear to everyone. Language such as "Whereupon, on motion duly made, seconded and carried, it was resolved that..." will usually be enough for the minutes to indicate how the matter was handled at the meeting.

6. Each action taken at the meeting should be described in sufficient detail to eliminate ambiguity and disputes over exactly what was agreed upon at the meeting. This is perhaps the most important part of your recordkeeping chores. Most of the forms in this book are designed to provide a careful and accurate description of corporate actions by shareholders and directors. As noted earlier, about the only action these groups can legally take is to pass a resolution of one sort or another. However, it is the existence and functioning of the shareholders and directors that mark the difference between a corporation and a proprietorship. *The Corporate Forms Kit* gives you the generally accepted language for the most commonly used resolutions in corporate practice.

7. Every meeting that has a beginning should also have an end. The end of each meeting should be recorded in the minutes and followed by the signature of the chairperson and secretary of the meeting.

Forms for the minutes of a regular and a special meeting of shareholders are contained in Chapter 2. At the beginning of this and every other chapter of the book is a set of instructions describing each form and explaining its use. If the use of one form requires the use of a companion or supplementary form, this is noted in the instructions. With this recordkeeping system, you have at your fingertips all the pertinent documents you will ordinarily need to do business as a corporation.

Chapter 3 contains forms for specific resolutions that may be adopted by the shareholders. Depending on the nature of the subject matter, shareholder approval may or may not be required. The system employed in this book is to include shareholder resolutions for two types of actions:

1. Those for which the law requires shareholder approval, e.g., a proposed merger
2. Those for which it is considered better practice to obtain shareholder approval, e.g., the adoption of an employee benefit plan

With this recordkeeping system, therefore, you have all the pertinent documents you will ordinarily need to record the proper and lawful activities of your corporation's shareholders.

The Record of Directors' Meetings—The Book of Minutes

Most of the rules and procedures that apply to shareholders' meetings apply equally to meetings of the board of directors. The single most important difference is who is qualified to vote on a particular matter. With shareholders, voting is a cut-and-dried affair. If they own common stock, they have the right to vote on any matter that comes before the shareholders. Not so with directors. Directors who have an interest in a matter to be voted upon by the board of directors should not vote on the matter. If an interested director does vote, the matter can be voided by the corporation or by the shareholders unless the interested director can demonstrate in court that the transaction was entirely fair to the corporation.

Virtually every state statute provides that a director with a personal interest in the matter may be counted in determining whether a quorum exists, but two cautions should be observed:

1. The interested director should disclose all material information concerning his or her interest in the matter. Assume, for example, that the corporation wishes to purchase a truck owned by another corporation and that a member of the board of directors of the buying corporation owns shares in the selling corporation. That fact should be disclosed to the board of the buying corporation before it votes, along with the number or percentage of shares the director owns in the selling corporation.
2. The interested director's vote should not be included in determining whether a majority of the board approves of the transaction in question.

Of course, the board still has the responsibility to act in the company's best interests. The board cannot put the interests of an individual, even a sole shareholder, above the interests of the company. It is the tension between these interests that characterizes the central dilemma of the close corporation.

In practical terms, this means that the corporation's records should show that the actions of the board treat the corporation fairly and that the board has good reasons for the actions it takes. Especially in matters concerning dividends, compensation, contracts and loans to officers and shareholders, it is critically important for the minutes to contain all the arguments, reports, statistics and other documents that can help establish a "reasonable basis" for the board's actions. With respect to loans, it should be noted that almost every state prohibits a corporation from lending money to a director if that person is not also employed by the corporation in some other capacity, e.g., president, vice president or department manager.

Chapter 2 of this book contains the forms for the minutes of the first board meeting, as well as for regular meetings of the board. At the first meeting, the board normally adopts a host of resolutions pertaining to how the company will conduct its business: what bylaws will be adopted, where the company's principal offices will be located, the form of the corporate seal and stock certificates and so on. If any of these resolutions were not adopted by formal resolution at your corporation's first meeting of the board, you should consider doing so at the next board meeting.

Normally, the regular board meeting is concerned only with electing officers for the ensuing year, setting their salaries and other compensation and declaring dividends. Other actions by the board will require the use of special resolutions, which can be found beginning in Chapter 3, through the end of the kit. The same considerations that apply to selecting shareholder resolutions apply to the selection and use of board resolutions.

One of the main reasons for keeping records of formal resolutions is that you will occasionally get requests from outside entities such as banks, insurance companies or state agencies for official copies of board or shareholder resolutions. Some will also require an affidavit to be completed by the secretary to certify that the resolution is a true copy of the resolution actually adopted. For this reason, at the end of each form is the text of a standard secretary's certificate. The form has blanks for you to fill in with pertinent information and space to imprint the corporate seal, as well as a notary's seal and signature.

Properly used, *The Corporate Forms Kit* provides you with a simple, easy-to-use and legally sound records system for your corporation.

Standard Clauses

In order to provide you with as many forms as possible, three standard clauses that appear in many forms will be set out below. When they are needed in a form, they will be referred to by the legends that introduce them.

Secretary's Certificate # 1

This paragraph is used when the corporation's secretary must certify a resolution adopted by the board of directors. The language of the certification you must insert follows:

The undersigned, _____ , certifies that I am the duly appointed Secretary of _____ Corporation and that the above is a true and correct copy of a resolution duly adopted at a meeting of the directors thereof, convened and held in accordance with law and the Bylaws of said Corporation on _____ , 19___ , and that such resolution is now in full force and effect.

   IN WITNESS THEREOF, I have affixed my name as Secretary of _____ Corporation and have attached the seal of _____ Corporation to this resolution.

_____
Secretary

Dated: _____ , 19___ .

Secretary's Certificate # 2

This paragraph is used when the corporation's secretary must certify a resolution adopted by the corporation's shareholders. The language of the certification you must insert follows:

The undersigned, _____ , certifies that I am the duly appointed Secretary of _____ Corporation and that the above is a true and correct copy of a resolution duly adopted at a meeting of the shareholders thereof, convened and held in accordance with law and the Bylaws of said Corporation on _____ , 19___ , and that such resolution is now in full force and effect.

   IN WITNESS THEREOF, I have affixed my name as Secretary of _____ Corporation and have attached the seal of _____ Corporation to this resolution.

_____
Secretary

Dated: _____ , 19___ .

Time, Date and Location Clause

Whenever a directors' or shareholders' meeting is scheduled, a notice of that meeting should be sent to the appropriate persons. Although there is no prescribed format for setting out the time, date and location of a meeting, the following format is recommended because it is clear, direct and easily understood:

Time:
Date: , 19   .
Address:

CHAPTER 2

Minutes of Meetings

Shareholders' Meetings

Most corporate charters provide for an annual meeting of shareholders. Generally, the main business at shareholders' meetings is to elect a board of directors to serve for the ensuing year. It is also good practice for the shareholders to adopt a resolution ratifying all the acts taken by the board during the past year.

In addition, specific actions that require shareholder approval, such as an amendment to the articles of incorporation or a merger proposal, also may be taken at the annual meeting.

The procedure to be followed when calling a shareholders' meeting is rather standardized throughout the United States. First, the board should adopt a resolution in which it states where and when the meeting is to be held. Forms 101 and 151 offer formats for both regular and special meetings. Next, the board should set a record date, i.e., the date upon which a person must be a shareholder if he or she is to have the right to vote. (Persons acquiring shares after the record date may not vote at the meeting unless they obtain a proxy from the person who sold the shares to them.)

The board must then have a notice sent to shareholders. This notice must contain the time, date and place of the meeting, and it should list the known agenda for the meeting. (If a special meeting is to be held, the notice must state the purpose or purposes for which the meeting is being called.) Ample notice must be given;

most states provide that at least ten days' notice, and not more than either 50 or 60 days' notice, is to be provided. Occasionally, either the corporation's articles of incorporation or bylaws will specify a time period within those parameters; in such cases, the notice provision in the corporate document must be followed.

Should the board fail to send out a notice of the meeting, or should there be an emergency that does not allow for the satisfaction of the waiver of notice, Form 153 provides a waiver format.

A number of states provide that if a corporate action requires a shareholder vote, e.g., an amendment of the articles of incorporation, the action may be taken without holding a shareholders' meeting if (1) the corporation obtains a written consent to the action from the shareholders, and (2) the written consent sets out a statement of the action to which the shareholders have consented. Corporations can also use consents if there has been a breakdown or failure in the processes leading up to or taking place during a shareholders' meeting, or if through an oversight a meeting was not called and shareholder approval is needed. Where the states differ is in the number of shareholders who must sign a consent in order for it to be effective. Delaware, for example, requires the signatures of only a majority of the shareholders entitled to vote on the action, i.e., enough so that if a meeting had been held, the action would have been approved. Other states require the consent to be signed by all shareholders entitled to vote on the matter.

Board of Directors' Meetings

The same considerations that apply to keeping minutes of shareholders' meetings also apply to board meetings: The minutes record the time, place, attendance, agenda and actions taken by the board, together with all the reports, contracts and other documents relevant to the actions taken at the meeting.

At the very first meeting of directors, much of the procedure that the corporation will follow is established. The bylaws, the corporate seal, stock certificates and record books are adopted, and the company's business is launched. Form 201 contains the standard litany of resolutions commonly adopted at the first board meeting. If your corporation is an existing one, you *should* still check these resolutions to make sure that your company hasn't overlooked a vital step.

Unlike shareholders' meetings, the procedure for calling a board meeting is not quite so formal. As a rule, the articles of incorporation or bylaws of most corporations contain a provision that states when board meetings are to be held; those provisions constitute notice to each director. If neither the articles of incorporation nor the bylaws contain such a provision, every director must be given reasonable notice of a board meeting. Failure to supply each director with reasonable notice will invalidate the meeting.

Form 251 supplies the format for notice of a regular meeting of the board of directors. Form 252 is a standard format for the minutes of the annual board meeting. The main business of the annual meeting is to declare a dividend, elect officers for the ensuing year and set the salary of each officer. If the board takes any additional action, a record of it should be added to the minutes of the meeting, in basically the same format used for the minutes of shareholders' meetings.

Form 261 can be used to supply notice of a special meeting of the board. Form 262 sets out a format for the minutes of a special meeting of the board. In the event that adequate notice has not been given for either a regular or a special meeting, Form 263 sets out a format for waiver of notice by directors.

Although a proxy form (154) has been supplied for shareholders' meetings, there is no counterpart for directors' meetings. Most courts take the position that directors may not vote by proxy. A proxy is simply a form of agency whereby one person gives another person the right to cast his or her vote at a shareholders' meeting. Ordinarily a proxy is easily revocable. So, if the person who creates the proxy shows up at the meeting and seeks to vote, the proxy will be deemed to have been revoked. Similarly, a proxy can be revoked if the person who grants it subsequently gives his or her proxy to another person. In some instances, however, the person who receives the proxy can demand that it be made irrevocable. For example, a lender or creditor may be unwilling to lend additional money or extend further credit unless he or she receives an irrevocable proxy. Or, as quite commonly occurs, an individual has agreed to purchase a shareholder's interest and demands the right to vote those shares until the transfer actually takes place. One caution: Form 154, the proxy form, is designed solely for use by a small, closed corporation.

NOTICE OF ANNUAL SHAREHOLDERS' MEETING

Date: , 19   .

To the shareholders of   :

                          Corporation will hold its annual meeting of shareholders at the corporation's principal office on the date and at the time and address shown below:

[Add Time, Date and Location Clause (see p. 14).]

The shareholders will consider and take action on the following matters:

1. The election of   directors.
2. The transaction of any other business that may be brought properly before the meeting or any adjournment or adjournments thereof.

Shareholders of record at the close of business on   ,
19   , will be entitled to vote in person or by proxy at the meeting or any adjournment or adjournments thereof.

By Direction of the Board of Directors of

Corporation

_____

Secretary

BOARD OF DIRECTORS' RESOLUTION—
SETTING RECORD DATE

Upon a duly made and seconded motion, a majority of the directors of the Board of Directors of _____ Corporation voted to adopt the following resolution:

RESOLVED, that the record date for determining the identity of those shareholders who will be entitled to vote at the meeting of shareholders that has been called for the _____ day of _____ , 19 _____ , shall be the close of business of the _____ day of _____ , 19 _____ .

[Insert Secretary's Certificate #1 (see p. 13).]

_____
Secretary

MINUTES OF ANNUAL SHAREHOLDERS' MEETING

The annual meeting of shareholders of   for the year ending 19   was held at the following time and date and at the following location:

[Add Time, Date and Location Clause (see p. 14).]

The President of the Corporation, who also served as Chairperson of the meeting, called the meeting to order, and the Secretary submitted a copy of the notice of the meeting that was mailed to all shareholders of record on   , 19   , and an affidavit stating that the notice had been mailed, postage prepaid to each shareholder of record as of the close of business on   , 19   , at the address shown for each shareholder on the   Corporation's records. The Secretary was then directed to file the copy of the notice of the meeting and his or her affidavit with the minutes of the meeting. The Secretary was also directed to keep the record of the meeting.

The Secretary then reported that the following shareholders were present in person or were represented by proxy (proxies representing a shareholder are parenthetically identified in the list that follows):

Names   Number of Shares

_____   _____

_____   _____

_____   _____

and that the shareholders who were present in person or by proxy constituted both a quorum and a majority of all outstanding shares entitled to vote at the meeting.

The Secretary was then directed to file all proxies with the minutes of the meeting. The shareholder records of the Corporation were produced and remained open and available for inspection throughout the entire course of the meeting.

The Secretary read the minutes of the last meeting of shareholders; those minutes were approved as read by the shareholders in attendance after a duly made and seconded motion.

The President then announced that the next item of business to come before the meeting was the election of a Board of Directors to serve for the ensuing year.

The President then asked the shareholders in attendance for nominations for the Board of Directors. The following individuals were then nominated, and their nominations were duly seconded:

_____

_____

_____

There being no other nominations, the President stated that nominations were closed. The ballots of the shareholders were presented to the Secretary, who reported that   ,   and   had received a plurality of the votes cast by and in behalf of the shareholders.

The Chairperson then announced that   ,   and   were the duly elected directors of the   Corporation for the immediately following year.

The President then asked if there was any further old or new business any person in attendance wished to bring before the meeting. Whereupon no further business came before the meeting, and upon a duly made, seconded and carried motion, the meeting was adjourned.

_____
Secretary

NOTICE OF SPECIAL MEETING OF SHAREHOLDERS

Date: , 19   .

To the shareholders of   :

Corporation will hold a special meeting of shareholders at the following time and date and at the following location:

[Add Time, Date and Location Clause (see p. 14).]

The purpose of the meeting is to present to shareholders for their consideration, discussion and action the following resolution that was adopted by the Corporation's directors at its meeting of   , 19   :

Only those shareholders who were shareholders of record at the close of business on   , 19   , will be entitled to vote, in person or by proxy, at the meeting or any adjournment or adjournments thereof.

By the Direction of the Board of Directors

of   Corporation.

_____

Secretary

MINUTES OF SPECIAL MEETING OF SHAREHOLDERS

A special meeting of the shareholders of
Corporation was held at the following time, date and location:

[Add Time, Date and Location Clause (see p. 14).]

The President of the Corporation,   , called the
meeting to order, and   , the Secretary of the
Corporation, took the minutes of the meeting. The Secretary then read aloud the
notice of the meeting supplied to shareholders, and read aloud his or her affidavit
containing proof that the notice had been mailed to each shareholder of record on
                         , 19   , at least two weeks before the date of the meeting.
The Secretary was then directed to make the affidavit containing the proof of
mailing a part of the minutes of the meeting.

The Secretary reported that the following shareholders were present in person
or were represented by proxy (proxies representing shareholders are identified in
parentheses in the list that follows):

Names   Number of Shares

_____   _____

_____   _____

_____   _____

and that there was present, in person and represented by proxy, holders of a
sufficient number of shares necessary to constitute a quorum and to transact
business.

After a duly made and seconded motion, and after due deliberation, the
following resolution was adopted by the affirmative vote of the holders of a
majority of the outstanding shares of stock entitled to vote:

The vote on the above resolution, the Secretary reported, showed that
over   percent of the outstanding shares entitled to vote had been cast and
that   shares of common stock had been voted in favor of the resolution and
that   shares of common stock had been voted against the resolution.

The President then announced that the resolution had been duly adopted by the holders of a majority of the shares entitled to vote on the resolution and that such majority was sufficient to transact the business of the meeting.

There being no further business, upon a duly made and seconded motion, the meeting was adjourned.

_____
Secretary

WAIVER OF NOTICE OF ANNUAL MEETING
(INDIVIDUAL SHAREHOLDER)

I, _____, the holder of _____ shares of stock of _____, Inc., do hereby waive notice of the annual meeting of the shareholders of _____, Inc., and consent to the holding of the meeting that is scheduled to be held on the following date and time and at the following location:

Date:

Time:

Suite:

Street:

City and state:

    I understand that the purposes of the meeting are to elect a new Board of Directors and that the agenda of the meeting may include the transaction of any other business that properly may be brought before the shareholders for their vote.

Dated: _____, 19 ___ .

                             _____
                             Signature

AUTHORIZATION (PROXY) TO VOTE SHARES

Date: , 19   .

    The undersigned, the record owner of

Corporation's Share Certificate No.   , representing   shares of stock in

the   Corporation, authorizes

to vote the aforementioned shares at the   Corporation's

shareholders' meeting to be held at the following time, date and location:

    [Add Time, Date and Location Clause (see p. 14).]

    By virtue of this proxy,   shall have the right to

vote for the election of directors and on any other business that may be raised

properly at the meeting.

_____

                Signature

MINUTES OF FIRST DIRECTORS' MEETING

The Board of Directors of   Corporation held its first meeting on the   day of   , 19   , at   o'clock   .m. in the City of   , State of   .

The following directors, who constitute the entire Board of Directors, were present:

,

and   .

Upon a duly seconded and carried motion,   was elected Acting Chairperson, and   was elected Acting Secretary of the meeting.

The Secretary then read aloud a waiver of notice of the meeting, which was signed by all of the directors. Upon a duly made and seconded and carried motion, the Secretary was ordered to attach the waiver with the minutes of the meeting.

The Secretary then distributed copies of the minutes of the meeting of incorporators and subscribers to the capital stock of the Corporation. Upon a duly made and seconded motion, those minutes were approved and the Secretary was ordered to attach them to the minutes of this meeting.

Next, upon a duly made, seconded and carried motion, the Board of Directors RESOLVED, that the acts of   and   , the incorporators of   Corporation, taken both jointly and severally on behalf of the Corporation are hereby approved, ratified and adopted as acts of the Corporation.

Next, the following individuals were nominated to serve as officers of the Corporation:

                   , President;
                   , Vice President;
                   , Secretary;
                   , Treasurer.

The directors then voted on the nominations and each of the nominated individuals was elected to the office that appears after his or her name.

Next, upon a duly made, seconded and carried motion, it was

RESOLVED, that the share certificates of this Corporation shall be those submitted by the President for consideration by the Board, and that a copy of said share certificate shall be attached to the minutes of this meeting.

Next, upon a duly made, seconded and carried motion, it was

RESOLVED, that the officers of the Corporation are hereby authorized and directed to pay all fees and expenses incident and necessary to the organization of the Corporation and to procure and pay for the proper corporate books.

Upon a motion duly made, seconded and carried, it was

RESOLVED, that the seal of the Corporation shall be the seal an impression of which appears immediately below:

(SEAL)

Next, upon a duly made, seconded and carried motion, it was

RESOLVED, that the Secretary is hereby authorized to procure for the Corporation all necessary books and the Treasurer is hereby authorized to pay all fees and other expenses incident and necessary to the Corporation's organization.

Next, a copy of the proposed Bylaws for the management of the Corporation's internal affairs was distributed to each director and read aloud. Then, upon a duly made, seconded and carried motion, it was

RESOLVED, that the Bylaws for the management of the internal affairs of the Corporation, which each director has read and approved article by article, are hereby adopted, and the Secretary is ordered to attach a copy of the aforesaid Bylaws to the minutes of this meeting.

Next, upon a motion duly made, seconded and carried, it was

RESOLVED, that the President of the Corporation is hereby authorized and directed to open a bank account in the Corporation's name and to do so in accordance with the form of bank resolution that is attached to the minutes of this meeting.

Next, the Board of Directors reviewed offers from   ,
to pay   dollars ($) in consideration for the issuance of
      shares of the common stock of the Corporation to be issued as fully paid and
nonassessable and from   , to pay
dollars ($) in consideration for the issuance of   shares of the
common stock of the Corporation to be issued as fully paid and nonassessable.

Next, upon a duly made, seconded and carried motion, it was

RESOLVED, that the aforesaid offers by   and
                              were for good and sufficient consideration for the
shares demanded, and it was

FURTHER RESOLVED, that the President and Secretary are hereby directed
to execute in the name of the Corporation any agreement or agreements in
accordance with the offers of   and
              and to issue and deliver in accordance with such an agreement or
agreements the appropriate number of fully paid and nonassessable shares.

RESOLVED, that the stock and stock transfer book recommended to the
Board at this meeting by the President are hereby adopted as the stock and stock
transfer book of the Corporation.

Next, upon a duly made, seconded and carried motion, it was

RESOLVED, that the firm of   be engaged to
perform the annual audit of the books of this Corporation for the calendar year
ending   , 19   and that the President is hereby authorized
and directed to execute a written retainer for the aforesaid services of

There being no further business, upon a duly made, seconded and carried
motion, the meeting was adjourned.

_____
Secretary

NOTICE OF DIRECTORS' MEETING

To:

     In accordance with the Bylaws of   , a meeting of the Board of Directors of   will be held at

o'clock   .m., on the   day of   , 19   , in the offices of

the   Corporation at   in the

City of   .

Dated: , 19   .

MINUTES OF DIRECTORS' MEETING

The Board of Directors of   held a regular meeting at the following time, date and place:

[Add Time, Date and Location Clause (see p. 14).]

The following individuals, constituting the entire membership of the Board of Directors, were present at the meeting:

                                        , the Corporation's President, chaired the meeting, and   , the Corporation's Secretary, served as Secretary of the meeting.

The Secretary read a waiver of notice of the meeting that was signed by all of the directors and was directed to attach the waiver of notice to the minutes of the meeting.

The Chairperson announced that a quorum of the directors was present and that the meeting could proceed with business. The Secretary distributed copies of the minutes of the previous regular meeting of the directors that had been held on   , 19   , and upon a duly made and seconded motion, the minutes of the aforesaid previous regular meeting were approved.

Next, the Board heard the report of   , the Corporation's Treasurer, which included the report of   , the Corporation's accountant, and was advised that as of the close of business on the   day of   , 19   , the Corporation had net profits of   dollars ($).

It was then

RESOLVED, that a dividend of   cents per share is hereby declared on the outstanding common stock of this Corporation, the said dividend to be payable to shareholders of record at the close of business on the   day of   , 19   , and shall be paid on the   day of   , 19   , and it is

FURTHER RESOLVED, that the Secretary is hereby directed to notify the shareholders that the dividend has been declared, and the Treasurer is hereby directed to pay the said dividend on the date specified above.

Next, the Board considered the reappointment of
as President of the Corporation.   thereupon excused himself or herself from the meeting and   replaced him or her as the Acting Chair. Upon a motion duly made and seconded and unanimously carried, it was

RESOLVED, that the salary of the President of the Corporation is to be
                    dollars ($) per year, and that term for which his or her employment shall continue under this resolution shall be one year.

Next, upon the conclusion of the vote on the above-described resolution, the President returned to the room and resumed the office of Chair of the meeting.

Next, the Board considered a proposed agreement for the supply of
                              to the Corporation that had been negotiated by the President, and it was

RESOLVED, that the Corporation should accept the proposed agreement, dated   , 19   , a copy of which is attached to the minutes of this meeting, and by this Resolution directs the President to execute the aforesaid agreement.

As no other business was before the meeting, a duly made and seconded motion to adjourn was carried.

_____

Chairperson

_____

Secretary

NOTICE OF SPECIAL MEETING OF DIRECTORS

The Board of Directors of   will hold a special meeting on the   day of   , 19   , at   o'clock,   .m., in the offices of the Corporation at   , in the City of   , to consider the following matter:

Dated: , 19   .

_____
Secretary

MINUTES OF SPECIAL MEETING OF DIRECTORS

The Board of Directors of   held a special meeting at the offices of the Corporation, located at   , in the City of   , in the State of   , on   , 19   , at   o'clock   .m. The following persons, constituting the entire membership of the directors of the Corporation, were present:

, served as Chairperson of the meeting, and served as Secretary of the meeting. After reading a waiver of notice of the meeting's notice, which had been signed by every director, the Secretary was directed to attach a copy of the waiver with the minutes of the meeting.

Having announced that a quorum of the Board of Directors, as required by the Bylaws of the Corporation, necessary for the holding of a meeting of the directors was present and that the meeting had been duly convened, the Chairperson further announced that the meeting could proceed with its business.

Upon a duly made, seconded and fully discussed motion, the following resolution was adopted:

There being no further business before the meeting, on the motion of   , seconded and carried, the meeting was adjourned.

_____
Secretary

WAIVER OF NOTICE OF DIRECTORS' MEETING

Dated: , 19   .

    The undersigned, each a member of the Board of Directors of the
                              Corporation, hereby waive notice of and consent to
the holding of the meeting of the Board of Directors of the Corporation scheduled
to be held at   o'clock   .m., on the   day of   , 19   , at
the offices of the Corporation located at   in the City
of   , and hereby agree that any lawful business may be
transacted at the meeting.

                                       _____

                                       _____

                                       _____

DEMAND FOR INSPECTION OF BOOKS AND RECORDS

Date: , 19   .

To: , Secretary,   Corporation

Subject: Demand for Inspection of Corporation's Books and Records

The undersigned hereby states that he or she is the holder of   shares of the common stock of   Corporation, and that (1) that holding constitutes at least five percent of the outstanding stock of the Corporation and (2) the undersigned has held the aforementioned shares of stock for at least six months preceding this demand.

The undersigned does hereby demand the opportunity to inspect the books and records of the Corporation, its stock ledger and the list of shareholders. The undersigned's purpose is a proper purpose in that it is being made

The undersigned further states that he or she has never sold or offered for sale any list of shareholders of any corporation, nor has he or she aided, abetted or assisted any person in obtaining such a list or record for such purpose.

_____

Signature

_____

Notary Public

CHAPTER 3

Changes in Governance of Corporation

Amending Articles of Incorporation

The shareholders and directors must approve any amendment to the corporation's articles of incorporation, and the state of incorporation must be notified of all amendments. Normally, the board will send a notice of a shareholders' meeting to each shareholder, and the notice will contain a draft of the resolution to adopt the amendment. Form 1100 can be used for this notice. Shareholder approval of the amendment can be recorded on Form 1101.

It is good practice to obtain a record of the written consent of each shareholder to the amendment, and Form 1102 can be used for this purpose.

Once the shareholders approve the amendment, the board should pass a resolution formally adopting the amendment and record it in the book of minutes. Form 1103 contains this resolution.

Finally, the Secretary of State of the state of incorporation normally requires a certificate of amendment to be filed for the amendment to become effective. The standard format for this certificate is shown in Form 1104. This form is to be filed with the Secretary of State in the state in which you have incorporated. Some states also require a notarized affidavit verifying the number of outstanding shares, as shown in Form 1105.

Perhaps the three most common reasons for amending the articles of incorporation are as follows:

1. To change the name of the corporation (Form 1110 can serve this purpose). This form is filed with the Secretary of State.
2. To increase the capital stock of the corporation (Form 1111). This form is filed with the Secretary of State.
3. To change the address of a corporation's principal place of business (Form 1112). This form is filed with the Secretary of State.

Any of these actions, as with any other change in the articles of incorporation, normally will require the usage of Forms 1100 through 1105.

Amending Bylaws

Just as with amendments of the articles of incorporation, amendments of the bylaws require approval of the shareholders and the board of directors. Thus, Form 1120 can be used by the board to send a draft of the amendment to the shareholders, along with the notice of the shareholders' meeting. Shareholder consent to the amendment can be recorded on Form 1121.

The hassle of calling a shareholders' meeting can be avoided if the shareholders adopt the resolution on Form 1122, which gives the board unlimited power to amend the bylaws. However, this resolution also specifies that the shareholders reserve the right to revoke or change any bylaw amendment that the board adopts.

Changes in Membership of Board of Directors

Form 1130 can be used to fill any vacancy on the board until the next annual shareholders' meeting, when the regular election of directors is held.

If a member of the board resigns, Form 1131 can be used to formally accept the resignation. Likewise, if the board wishes to remove a director, it can adopt the resolution on Form 1132, which requests a director or officer to submit his or her resignation. The resolution on Form 1133 is more direct, however, and serves to remove an officer or director without asking for his or her resignation. When an officer or director is removed without being given an opportunity to resign, it is customary to send him or her formal notice, such as that contained in Form 1134.

BOARD OF DIRECTORS' RESOLUTION ADVISING OF AMENDMENT TO ARTICLES OF INCORPORATION

By a duly made and seconded motion, a majority of the directors of the Board of Directors of _____ Corporation, voted to adopt the following resolution:

RESOLVED, that the Board of Directors of the Corporation finds it in the best interests of the Corporation to amend Article _____ of the Articles of Incorporation to read as follows:

And it is

FURTHER RESOLVED, that the President of the Corporation call a special meeting of the Corporation's shareholders, to be held at _____ on _____, 19__ at ____.m., to consider and vote upon the above resolution, and the President of the Corporation is directed to require the Corporation's Secretary to give notice of the special meeting to shareholders in accordance with the Corporation's Bylaws.

[Insert Secretary's Certificate #1 (see p. 13).]

(SEAL)

SHAREHOLDERS' RESOLUTION APPROVING AMENDMENT TO ARTICLES OF INCORPORATION

WHEREAS, the Board of Directors of
Corporation has voted in favor of amending Article   , Section   , of the
Corporation's Articles of Incorporation as set forth below, and

WHEREAS, the shareholders of the   Corporation
approve of that amendment, it is hereby

RESOLVED, that Article   of the Corporation's Articles of Incorporation
is amended and shall now provide that:

It is

FURTHER RESOLVED, that the shareholders authorize and direct the
Chairperson and Secretary of this meeting to prepare a sealed certificate setting
out the above resolution and to do everything necessary for the certificate to be
filed with the appropriate State office.

It is

FURTHER RESOLVED, that a duplicate copy of the amendment as returned
by the appropriate State official shall be attached to the minutes of this meeting.

[Insert Secretary's Certificate #2 (see p. 13).]

(SEAL)

SHAREHOLDERS' CERTIFICATE OF CONSENT TO AMENDMENT TO ARTICLES OF INCORPORATION

The undersigned, the shareholders of _____ Corporation, by this certificate consent and adopt as an amendment to the Articles of Incorporation of this Corporation the proposal set out and adopted by the directors of the Corporation in their resolution of _____ , 19___ , the language of which immediately follows:

Shareholder   Number of Shares

_____   _____

_____   _____

_____   _____

_____   _____

_____
Secretary

BOARD OF DIRECTORS' RESOLUTION ADOPTING AMENDMENT TO ARTICLES OF INCORPORATION

WHEREAS, the shareholders of   Corporation have given their written consent and authorization for the Board of Directors of   Corporation to amend Article   of the Articles of Incorporation, and

WHEREAS, the written consent of the shareholders is now on file in the Corporation's minute book, the Board of Directors of   Corporation has hereby

RESOLVED, that Article   of the Articles of Incorporation is amended and now provides that:

[Insert Secretary's Certificate #1 (see p. 13).]
(SEAL)

CERTIFICATE OF AMENDMENT TO ARTICLES
OF INCORPORATION

_____

_____, Inc., a Corporation formed under Section

of the _____ Law of the State of _____ .

   The undersigned, the President and the Secretary of _____

Corporation certify that at a shareholders' meeting held on _____ ,

19____ , and which was called for the purpose of amending the Articles of

Incorporation of _____ Corporation, an appropriate majority

of the holders of shares of each class entitled to vote authorized the following

amendment of Article ____ of the Articles of Incorporation:

Dated: _____ , 19____ .

                                   ,Inc.

        By _____

        President

        _____

        Secretary

SECRETARY'S AFFIDAVIT VERIFYING NUMBER OF OUTSTANDING SHARES

State of

County of

$\Big\}$ ss:

, who has been duly sworn and deposes, says:

1. That he/she is the duly appointed Secretary of
   Corporation, which was organized and currently exists under the laws of
   the State of   .

2. That as of this day,   Corporation currently
   has   shares of the stock issued and outstanding and that the
   amendment of Article   of the Articles of Incorporation of the
                                   Corporation, attached hereto, was authorized
   by a vote of the holders of a majority of the shares of each class entitled to
   vote thereon at a duly called meeting of shareholders.

   Sworn to in my presence on this the   day of   , 19   .

   _____
   Secretary

_____
Notary Public
   (SEAL)

SHAREHOLDERS' RESOLUTION CHANGING NAME OF CORPORATION

Upon a duly made and seconded motion, the resolution that follows below was duly adopted by the holders of a majority of the shares entitled to vote on the resolution:

RESOLVED, that the name of the   Corporation is changed to   , and it is

FURTHER RESOLVED, that the officers of the Corporation are hereby directed to file in the appropriate State office a certificate setting forth the change of name of the   Corporation to   Corporation.

[Insert Secretary's Certificate #2 (see p. 13).]

(SEAL)

SHAREHOLDERS' RESOLUTION INCREASING CAPITAL STOCK

Upon a duly made and seconded motion, the following resolution was duly adopted by the holders of a majority of the shares entitled to vote:

RESOLVED, that Corporation's authorized capital stock which is now
      dollars ($), and which consists of   shares, each having a par value of   dollars ($), is hereby increased to a total authorized capital stock of   dollars ($), consisting of   shares, each having a par value of   dollars ($), and it is

FURTHER RESOLVED, that the Corporation's officers are hereby directed to file in the appropriate State office a certificate setting forth the above change in the Corporation's capital stock.

[Insert Secretary's Certificate #2 (see p. 13).]

(SEAL)

SHAREHOLDERS' RESOLUTION CHANGING CORPORATION ADDRESS

Upon a duly made and seconded motion, the following resolution was duly adopted by the holders of a majority of the shares entitled to vote:

RESOLVED, that the address of the   Corporation's principal office is to be changed from   Street, in the County of   , in the State of   , to   Street in the County of   , in the State of   , and it is

FURTHER RESOLVED, that the officers of the Corporation are hereby directed to file in the appropriate State office a certificate setting forth the above change of address.

[Insert Secretary's Certificate #2 (see p. 13).]
(SEAL)

BOARD OF DIRECTORS' RESOLUTION ADVISING AMENDMENT OF BYLAWS

Upon a duly made and seconded motion, the resolution that follows below was duly adopted by the directors: RESOLVED, that Section   of the Bylaws of the Corporation be changed to read as follows:

And it is

FURTHER RESOLVED, that the President of the Corporation is hereby directed to convene a special meeting of the shareholders of the   Corporation on   , 19   , at   .m. to consider and take action on the above proposed amendment of the Bylaws of the   Corporation.

[Insert Secretary's Certificate #1 (see p. 13).]

(SEAL)

CERTIFICATE OF SHAREHOLDERS' CONSENT TO AMENDMENT OF BYLAWS

The undersigned, who comprise all of the shareholders of
Corporation, do hereby signify our consent to the
following resolution adopted by the Board of Directors of the
Corporation at duly convened meeting of the Board
that was held on   , 19   :

Shareholders' Signature   Number of Shares

_____   _____

_____   _____

_____   _____

Dated: , 19   .

SHAREHOLDERS' RESOLUTION ON BOARD OF DIRECTORS' AUTHORITY TO AMEND BYLAWS

RESOLVED, that the Board of Directors of
Corporation is hereby granted the authority to amend, alter, add to, repeal, rescind or change in any other way any and all of the Bylaws of this Corporation as the Board of Directors shall deem fit and proper, and such authority shall not require either any action or consent by or from the shareholders of the
Corporation; and it is

FURTHER RESOLVED, that the shareholders are to retain the right to revoke the above grant of authority to the directors. Such revocation shall be made by a resolution adopted by the holders of a majority of the
Corporation's stock entitled to vote at a duly convened meeting of shareholders. Unless and until such revocation action is taken by the shareholders, the shareholders shall not exercise their power, under Article   of the Bylaws to amend, alter, add to, repeal, rescind or change in any way the Bylaws of the
Corporation.

[Insert Secretary's Certificate #2 (see p. 13).]
(SEAL)

BOARD OF DIRECTORS' RESOLUTION FILLING VACANCY ON BOARD

Upon a motion that was duly made and seconded, the resolution that appears below was adopted by a vote of a majority of the Board of Directors:

RESOLVED, that   is hereby appointed to fill the vacancy on the Board of Directors created by the   and shall serve as a director of   Corporation until the next annual shareholders' meeting.

[Insert Secretary's Certificate #1 (see p. 13).]
(SEAL)

BOARD OF DIRECTORS' RESOLUTION ACCEPTING DIRECTOR'S RESIGNATION

Upon a duly made and seconded motion, a majority of the directors of the Board of Directors of   Corporation voted in favor of the following resolution:

RESOLVED, that the Board of Directors of   Corporation does hereby accept   's resignation from the Board of Directors of   Corporation, as stated by aforesaid   in his/her letter to the Board of Directors dated   , 19   . The Secretary of the Corporation is hereby instructed to notify M   .   that the Board has accepted his/her resignation.

[Insert Secretary's Certificate #1 (see p. 13).]
(SEAL)

BOARD OF DIRECTORS' RESOLUTION REQUESTING RESIGNATION OF OFFICER

Upon a duly made and seconded motion, a majority of the Directors of the

Corporation voted in favor of the following

resolution:

RESOLVED, that the Board of Directors of

Corporation hereby requests M   .   's resignation

from the office of   of

Corporation. It is

FURTHER RESOLVED, that the Secretary of the

Corporation is hereby directed to forward by certified mail a sealed copy of this

resolution to M   .   .

[Insert Secretary's Certificate #1 (see p. 13).]

(SEAL)

BOARD OF DIRECTORS' RESOLUTION REMOVING AN OFFICER OR DIRECTOR

Upon a duly made and seconded motion, a majority of the directors of the Board of Directors of _____ Corporation voted to adopt the following resolution:

RESOLVED, that M_____._____ is hereby removed from his/her office as _____ of this Corporation effective immediately. It is

FURTHER RESOLVED that the Secretary of this Corporation is hereby directed to give notice to M_____._____ of the fact that he/she has been removed from his/her office as _____ of _____ Corporation, and to provide such notice by means of sealed copies of this resolution sent to M_____._____ by interoffice mail and to his/her residence by certified mail.

[Insert Secretary's Certificate #1 (see p. 13).]

(SEAL)

NOTICE TO OFFICER OF REMOVAL BY BOARD

Dated: , 19   .

To   :

    This is to advise you that, pursuant to Section   of the Bylaws of
                          Corporation, the Board of Directors has removed you
from your position as   of the
    Corporation.

    The Board's action, taken by means of a resolution voted upon at a meeting
held on   , 19   , removed you from office as of the time of
the vote.

    A sealed copy of the resolution is attached to this notice; the original is on file
in the principal office of the Corporation.

_____
        Secretary

CHAPTER 4

Major Business Actions

Introduction

The forms in this section can be used to record major decisions of the shareholders or the board. While a specific resolution may not be essential to give the action full legal force, the forms will show outside parties that the action was actually taken by and on behalf of the corporation. Often, a bank, court or another corporation will ask for evidence that an officer has been empowered to bind the company. Copies of the appropriate form will usually serve this purpose.

Contracts

Form 2110 can be used to designate the president (and/or other officers) as the only person with authority to make estimates, sign contracts or order materials on behalf of the corporation. This form prevents unauthorized employees from binding the company inadvertently. It spells out exactly who has the authority and what the procedure is for making a binding estimate or contract with your company.

Form 2111 is a board resolution authorizing the president to negotiate the terms of a particular contract.

Form 2112 is a board resolution approving the terms of a particular contract. It is good practice to attach a copy of the contract to minutes of the meeting at which the resolution was adopted.

Loans

Form 2120 can be used to authorize borrowing on a line of credit extended by a bank and evidenced by a promissory note. With this resolution, the note can be renewed without further action by the board. This resolution establishes a maximum limit on the amount that can be borrowed on the note.

Form 2121 authorizes corporate officers to set the amounts and terms of loans obtained from a particular bank. It gives the officers maximum discretion, allowing them to agree to any terms they may deem proper.

Form 2122 authorizes officers to obtain a loan by pledging inventory materials and other property as collateral. Form 2123 authorizes the pledging of accounts receivable as loan collateral.

Corporate Offices, Plant and Equipment

Form 2130 authorizes a lease. Landlords sometimes ask for evidence of this authority. Form 2140 actually authorizes two contracts: a sale of real estate, and a leaseback of that property. Form 2150 can be used by the board to authorize the purchase of land and improvements to be used for business purposes.

Appointment of Accountant or Attorney

Form 2160 authorizes the corporation to retain a new accounting firm. Form 2170 authorizes the appointment of an attorney to represent the corporation. Form 2171 authorizes the attorney to file a suit on behalf of the corporation; Form 2172 authorizes the attorney to defend the corporation in a suit filed against it.

Mergers

Form 2200 is a board resolution recommending that the shareholders approve the purchase of all the assets of another corporation and calling a shareholders' meeting for that purpose.

Form 2201 is a shareholders' resolution approving the purchase of all assets of another corporation. This agreement is filed with the Secretary of State.

Form 2201A sets out the format for the plan and agreement of a merger that has been proposed.

Form 2202 is a board resolution proposing to merge with a wholly owned subsidiary and calling a shareholders' meeting for that purpose.

Form 2203 is a shareholders' resolution approving the merger agreement.

Sale of Corporate Assets

Form 2210 is a shareholders' resolution giving the board blanket authority to sell all or part of the corporation's assets. Form 2220 is a board resolution accepting an offer to purchase all of the corporation's assets and calling a shareholders' meeting to approve that action. Form 2221 is a shareholders' resolution consenting to the sale of all corporate assets. It is customary to obtain the written consent of shareholders to a sale of all assets, and Form 2222 can be used for this purpose. (Note: Some states require a two-thirds majority of shareholders to consent to the sale of all or substantially all of the corporation's assets.)

Form 2223 authorizes the distribution to shareholders of the cash received from the sale of corporate assets and to announce a plan of liquidation.

Dissolution

Form 2230 recommends that the shareholders vote to dissolve the corporation and gives notice of a meeting to be held for that purpose.

Form 2231 is the shareholders' resolution consenting to dissolution and directing the officers to wind up the corporation's affairs.

Form 2232 is the Certificate of Dissolution filed with the Secretary of State.

Bankruptcy

Form 2240 is a board resolution recommending that the shareholders approve the filing of a bankruptcy petition and calling a shareholders' meeting.

BOARD OF DIRECTORS' RESOLUTION ON PRESIDENT'S AUTHORITY TO MAKE PURCHASES

Upon a duly made and seconded motion, a majority of the directors of the Board of Directors of _____ Corporation adopted the following resolutions:

RESOLVED, that estimates of the cost of any work to be performed by the _____ Corporation for third persons shall be prepared by or under the supervision of the President of the Corporation, and all completed estimates shall be retained by the Secretary in a file maintained solely to keep a record of all such estimates and no estimate shall be submitted by this Corporation unless it has been prepared by or approved by the President; and it is

FURTHER RESOLVED, that every order for (1) materials to be delivered to or (2) work or services to be performed for the Corporation shall be made in writing and shall not be valid unless it is signed by the President. Copies of all orders for materials, services or work shall be retained by the Secretary in a file maintained by the Secretary of the Corporation solely to keep a record of such orders.

[Insert Secretary's Certificate #1 (see p. 13).]

(SEAL)

BOARD OF DIRECTORS' RESOLUTION ON PRESIDENT'S AUTHORITY TO NEGOTIATE CONTRACT

Upon a duly made and seconded motion, a majority of the directors of the Board of Directors of   Corporation adopted the following resolution:

RESOLVED, that the President of   Corporation is hereby authorized to enter into a contract with the   Company for   , in the name and in behalf of this Corporation, and on the best terms and conditions the President can obtain from the   Company.

[Insert Secretary's Certificate #1 (see p. 13).]

BOARD OF DIRECTORS' RESOLUTION APPROVING
A PROPOSED CONTRACT

Upon a duly made and seconded motion, a majority of the directors of the Board of Directors of   Corporation adopted the following resolution:

WHEREAS, the President of   Corporation has submitted to the Board of Directors a proposed contract between this Corporation and   , dated   , 19   , which sets out the following terms:

and

WHEREAS, the Board of Directors has reviewed and discussed among themselves the above-described proposed contract, it is

RESOLVED, that the above-described contract is hereby approved by the Board of Directors, and the President of the Corporation is hereby authorized to enter into the said contract with   , in the name of and in behalf of this Corporation.

[Insert Secretary's Certificate #1 (see p. 13).]

(SEAL)

BOARD OF DIRECTORS' RESOLUTION APPROVING CREDIT LINE

Upon a duly made, seconded and carried motion, the Board of Directors of _____ Corporation, by unanimous vote, adopted the following resolution:

RESOLVED, that the President of this Corporation is hereby authorized to establish for the Corporation a credit line in the sum of _____ dollars ($ _____), from the _____ Bank, for and in behalf of this Corporation, on the terms set out in the Revolving Credit Agreement prepared by the _____ Bank and attached to the minutes of this meeting.

[Insert Secretary's Certificate #1 (see p. 13).]
(SEAL)

BOARD OF DIRECTORS' RESOLUTION FOR BORROWING FROM DESIGNATED BANK

WHEREAS, it has become necessary for this Corporation to borrow money in order to

it is hereby

RESOLVED, that   , the President of the Corporation, is hereby authorized to act for this Corporation and borrow from the   Bank of   the sum of   dollars ($) on the terms set out in the loan instrument attached to the minutes of this meeting, and to sign and execute that document and whatever other documents as may be necessary or required by the   Bank to evidence such indebtedness from this Corporation to the   Bank; and it is

FURTHER RESOLVED, that the Secretary of the Corporation is to provide the   Bank with a certified copy of these resolutions.

[Insert Secretary's Certificate #1 (see p. 13).]

(SEAL)

SHAREHOLDERS' RESOLUTION FOR BORROWING ON INVENTORY AND EQUIPMENT

WHEREAS, the Board of Directors of
Corporation has determined that it is necessary for this Corporation to borrow
money and that the most favorable terms available can be obtained by offering
certain of the Corporation's furniture, fixtures and inventory as collateral for the
loan, it is hereby

RESOLVED, that   , the President of this
Corporation is hereby authorized to borrow the sum of   dollars
($) from   on the terms set out in the
Promissory Note attached to the minutes of this meeting and to execute a
mortgage in favor of the Lender covering the furniture, fixtures and the inventory
of merchandise set out in the Schedule attached to the minutes of this meeting, and
it is

FURTHER RESOLVED, that the President of the Corporation is hereby
authorized and directed to provide for creditors of the Corporation all notices
required by law to be given to the creditors of the Corporation and to do
everything else that may be necessary to complete the transaction authorized by
the Board of Directors in this resolution.

[Insert Secretary's Certificate #2 (see p. 13).]

(SEAL)

SHAREHOLDERS' RESOLUTION FOR BORROWING ON ACCOUNTS RECEIVABLE

WHEREAS, the Board of Directors of this Corporation has determined that it has become necessary to borrow money for corporate purposes and that such funds can be obtained at favorable rates only by borrowing against the accounts receivable of the Corporation, it is hereby

RESOLVED, that the Board of Directors of this Corporation is hereby authorized to borrow   dollars ($) on the terms and conditions set out in the Promissory Note and Pledge Instruments attached to the minutes of this meeting.

[Insert Secretary's Certificate #2 (see p. 13).]

(SEAL)

BOARD OF DIRECTORS' RESOLUTION FOR LEASING CORPORATE OFFICES

WHEREAS, the Board of Directors of
Corporation has been informed that the landlord of the premises now occupied by
the   Corporation under a lease entered into by the
President of this Corporation with full authority of this Board of Directors has
informed the President of the Corporation that it requires evidence that the
Corporation accepts the terms of the lease, it is hereby

RESOLVED, that the Board of Directors hereby reaffirms the authority it
invested in   , the President of this Corporation, to enter
into the lease, a copy of which is attached to the minutes of this meeting, and to do
everything necessary to make the lease binding on this Corporation as tenant and
                              , as landlord.

[Insert Secretary's Certificate #1 (see p. 13).]

(SEAL)

BOARD OF DIRECTORS' RESOLUTION FOR SALE AND LEASEBACK OF REAL ESTATE

WHEREAS, the Board of Directors has determined that it will be in the best interests of the _____ Corporation to sell certain of its real property and to lease the same back from the purchasers, it is hereby

RESOLVED, that this Corporation sell the parcel of real property it owns and that is located at _____ , in the City of _____ , in the State of _____ , and that is described in the Deed attached to the minutes of this meeting, to the _____ Company, on the terms set out in the attached Deed, and that concurrently with that transfer, the Corporation shall take back a lease thereof from _____ , the buyer, on the terms set out in the Lease attached to the minutes of this meeting; and it is

FURTHER RESOLVED, that the President and Secretary of this Corporation are hereby authorized to act in behalf of the Corporation and to execute and deliver the Deed, Lease and such other instruments as may be required in connection with the sale and leaseback of the above mentioned real estate and to affix the corporate seal of this Corporation to such documents.

[Insert Secretary's Certificate #1 (see p. 13).]

(SEAL)

BOARD OF DIRECTORS' RESOLUTION FOR PURCHASE OF REAL ESTATE AND IMPROVEMENTS

WHEREAS, the   Corporation's operations now require additional operating facilities, and,

WHEREAS,   , the owner of the real estate located at   , in the City of   , State of   , has offered to sell that property to the Corporation on the terms and conditions set out in the Deed attached to the minutes of this meeting, it is hereby

RESOLVED, that this Corporation purchase from the land and building described in the Deed that is attached to the minutes of this meeting on the terms described in that Deed; and it is

FURTHER RESOLVED, that the President and Secretary of this Corporation are hereby authorized to execute all instruments and make all payments necessary to complete the sale of the aforementioned real estate to this Corporation.

[Insert Secretary's Certificate #1 (see p. 13).]

(SEAL)

BOARD OF DIRECTORS' RESOLUTION FOR
ENGAGING NEW ACCOUNTANT

RESOLVED, that, on   , 19   , when the contract
between this Corporation and the firm of   , the auditors
for this Corporation, shall expire, the said contract of employment of the firm of
                              shall not be renewed, and it is

FURTHER RESOLVED, that the President of this Corporation is hereby
authorized to enter into the Letter of Agreement submitted by the firm of
                              , on the terms and conditions set out in that letter, a
copy of which is attached to the minutes of this meeting.

[Insert Secretary's Certificate #1 (see p. 13).]

(SEAL)

BOARD OF DIRECTORS' RESOLUTION FOR APPOINTMENT OF ATTORNEYS

RESOLVED, that the President of this Corporation is hereby authorized to engage the law firm of   to serve as attorneys for this Corporation, on the terms and conditions set out in the Letter of Agreement dated   , 19   , and submitted to the Corporation by the aforementioned law firm, a copy of which is attached to the minutes of this meeting.

[Insert Secretary's Certificate #1 (see p. 13).]

(SEAL)

BOARD OF DIRECTORS' RESOLUTION
AUTHORIZING LITIGATION

WHEREAS,   has owed the

Corporation   dollars ($) for

delivered to the aforementioned on   , 19   ,

and has resisted every attempt of this Corporation's officers to collect such debt, it

is hereby

RESOLVED, that the law firm of   is hereby

authorized to initiate suit in the name of and in behalf of this Corporation to

satisfy its claim against   or to enter a settlement of the

claim at such amount and upon such terms as the President of this Corporation

agrees are appropriate.

[Insert Secretary's Certificate #1 (see p. 13).]

(SEAL)

BOARD OF DIRECTORS' RESOLUTION AUTHORIZING
ATTORNEY TO DEFEND CORPORATION AGAINST A CLAIM

WHEREAS, a claim against this Corporation has been presented by

and

WHEREAS, it appears that the aforesaid claim is without merit, it is hereby

RESOLVED, that the law firm of   is hereby

authorized to defend this Corporation against the meritless claim presented by

, and to take whatever actions they consider necessary

and appropriate to defend this Corporation, subject to the consent of the President

of this Corporation.

[Insert Secretary's Certificate #1 (see p. 13).]

(SEAL)

BOARD OF DIRECTORS' RESOLUTION ADVISING APPROVAL OF MERGER

WHEREAS, in the judgment of the Board of Directors of this Corporation it is deemed advisable to adopt the Articles of Merger set forth below, it is hereby

RESOLVED, that the Board of Directors deems it advisable to adopt the Articles of Merger, set out below, under the terms of which the _____ Corporation would be merged into this Corporation; and it is

FURTHER RESOLVED, that a special meeting of the shareholders of this Corporation is hereby scheduled to be held at _____ , .m., on _____ , 19 ___ , to take action upon the proposed merger, and the Secretary is hereby instructed to give notice of this special meeting to the shareholders of this Corporation in accordance with the Corporation's Bylaws, and to include in that notice a copy of the Articles of Merger immediately following:

[Insert Secretary's Certificate #1 (see p. 13).]
(SEAL)

SHAREHOLDERS' RESOLUTION APPROVING PURCHASE OF ALL ASSETS OF DESIGNATED CORPORATION

RESOLVED, that the Board of Directors of this Corporation is hereby authorized to acquire from   all its property, assets, accounts, receivables and goodwill on the terms and conditions set out in an agreement dated   , 19   , and attached to the minutes of this meeting.

[Insert Secretary's Certificate #2 (see p. 13).]

(SEAL)

PLAN AND AGREEMENT OF MERGER BETWEEN

_____

AND

_____

This Plan and Agreement of Merger is made and entered into on the   day of   , 19   , by and between   , a Corporation, hereinafter referred to as the Surviving Corporation, and   , a Corporation, hereinafter referred to as the Merged Corporation, and said Corporations are hereinafter sometimes referred to jointly as the Constituent Corporations.

WITNESSETH:

WHEREAS, the Surviving Corporation is organized and exists under the laws of the State of   , having filed its Certificate of Incorporation in the Office of the Secretary of State of the State of   on   , 19   , and recorded in the office of the Recorder of Deeds for the County of   , in the aforesaid State, on   , 19   , and having its registered office at   , in the City of   , County of   , and having as its registered agent   ; and

WHEREAS the total number of shares of stock which the Surviving Corporation has authority to issue is   shares, of which   shares are now issued and outstanding; and

WHEREAS, the Merged Corporation is organized and exists under the laws of the State of   , its Articles of Incorporation having been filed in the office of the Secretary of State of the State of   on the   day of   , 19   , and its Certificate of Incorporation, after being issued to the Merged Corporation by the Secretary of State on that date, was recorded in the office of the Recorder of Deeds of   County,   , on the   day of   , 19   , and the address of its registered office is   , in the County of   in the State of   , and its registered agent being   ; and

WHEREAS, the aggregate number of shares which the Merged Corporation has authority to issue is   shares, of which   shares are issued and outstanding; and

WHEREAS, the Board of Directors of each of the Constituent Corporations deems it advisable that the Merged Corporation be merged into the Surviving Corporation on the terms and conditions set forth below, in accordance with the applicable provisions of the statutes of the States of and   , respectively, which permit such merger;

THEREFORE, in consideration of the agreements, covenants and provisions set out below, the Surviving Corporation and the Merged Corporation, by their Boards of Directors, do hereby agree as follows:

ARTICLE I

The Surviving Corporation and the Merged Corporation shall be merged into a single corporation, in accordance with applicable provisions of the laws of the State of   and of the State of   , by the Merged Corporation merging into the Surviving Corporation, which shall be the Surviving Corporation.

ARTICLE II

Upon the merger becoming effective under the laws of the States of   and   (such time being referred to herein as the "Effective Date of the Merger"):

1. The two Constituent Corporations shall be a single corporation, which shall be the Surviving Corporation, and the separate existence of the Merged Corporation shall cease, except to the extent, if any, provided by the laws of the State of   .

2. The Surviving Corporation shall thereupon possess all the rights, privileges, immunities and franchises of the Constituent Corporations; and all property, real and personal, and all debts due on whatever account and every other interest belonging to or due to each of the Constituent Corporations shall be vested in the Surviving Corporation without further act or deed.

3. The Surviving Corporation shall be responsible and liable for all of the liabilities and obligations of each Constituent Corporation and all existing or pending claims, actions or proceedings by or against the Constituent

Corporations may be prosecuted to judgment as if the merger had not taken place, or the Surviving Corporation may be substituted in the place of the appropriate Constituent Corporation, and neither the rights of creditors nor any liens upon the property of the Constituent Corporations shall be impaired by the merger.

4. The Surviving Corporation hereby agrees that it may be served with process in the State of   in any proceeding for the enforcement of any obligation of either Constituent Corporation, including those arising from the merger, and hereby irrevocably appoints the Secretary of State of   as its agent to accept service of process in any such suit or other proceedings, and further agrees that service of any such process may be made by providing the Secretary of State of the State of   with duplicate copies of such process; and the Surviving Corporation authorizes the aforesaid Secretary of State to send such process to it by registered mail directed to its registered office at

5. With respect to each Constituent Corporation, the aggregate amount of net assets of each Constituent Corporation that was available to support and pay dividends before the merger shall continue to be available for the payment of dividends by the Surviving Corporation, except to the extent that all or a portion of those net assets may be transferred to the stated capital of the Surviving Corporation.

6. The Bylaws of the Surviving Corporation as they existed immediately before the effective date of merger shall be the Bylaws of the Surviving Corporation.

7. The persons who will serve on the Board of Directors and as the officers of the Surviving Corporation shall be the same persons who served as directors and officers of the Surviving Corporation immediately before the effective date of the merger.

ARTICLE III

The Articles of Incorporation of the Surviving Corporation shall not be amended in any respect by reason of this Agreement of Merger and said Articles of Incorporation shall constitute the Articles of Incorporation of the Surviving Corporation unless or until it is subsequently amended by the action of the Board of Directors and shareholders; the said Articles of Incorporation are set forth in

Exhibit A attached hereto and are made a part of this Plan and Agreement of Merger.

ARTICLE IV

The shares of the Constituent Corporations shall be converted into shares of the Surviving Corporation in the following manner:

1. Each share of each Constituent Corporation shall be converted into fully paid and non-assessable share(s) of capital stock of the Surviving Corporation.

ARTICLE V

The Surviving Corporation shall pay all expenses incurred for the purpose of bringing this Agreement of Merger and the merger herein described into effect.

ARTICLE VI

If the Surviving Corporation shall have reason to request any further assignments, conveyances or other transfers that on the advice of counsel are necessary to vest in the Surviving Corporation title to any property or rights of either of the Constituent Corporations, the officers and directors of the appropriate Constituent Corporation shall execute any assignment, conveyance or transfer to vest such property or rights in the Surviving Corporation.

ARTICLE VII

This Plan and Agreement of Merger shall be submitted to the shareholders of each of the Constituent Corporations for consideration at a meeting of shareholders held in accordance with the Bylaws of each Constituent Corporation and with the laws of their state of incorporation, and upon (a) the approval by the shareholders of each Constituent Corporation, and (b) the subsequent execution, filing and recording of such documents shall then take effect and be the Plan of Merger of the Constituent Corporations.

This Plan and Agreement of Merger may be abandoned by (a) either of the Constituent Corporations by the action of its Board of Directors if such action is taken before the Plan and Agreement of Merger has been approved by the shareholders of the Constituent Corporation whose Board seeks abandonment, or (b) the mutual consent of the Constituent Corporations if their respective Boards of Directors each adopt a resolution abandoning the Plan and Agreement of Merger before the effective date of the merger.

IN WITNESS WHEREOF, each Constituent Corporation acting by the authority set out in resolutions adopted by its Board of Directors has directed this Plan and Agreement of Merger to be executed by the President and attested to by the Secretary of each Constituent Corporation, and to have the corporate seal of each Constituent Corporation affixed hereto.

Attest:

_____   _____
Secretary   President
Attest:

_____   _____
Secretary   President

THE ABOVE AGREEMENT OF MERGER, having been executed by the President and Secretary of each corporate party thereto and having been adopted separately by the shareholders of each corporate party thereto, in accordance with the provisions of the General Corporation Law of the State of _____ , and the fact having been certified on said Agreement of Merger by the Secretary of each corporate party thereto do now hereby execute the said Agreement of Merger under the corporate seals of their respective Corporations, by the authority of the directors and shareholders thereof, as the respective act, deed and agreement of each of said Corporation, on the   day of _____ , 19   .

_____   _____
Secretary   President

_____   _____
Secretary   President

I, _____ , Secretary of _____ , a corporation organized and existing under the laws of the State of _____ , hereby certify, as such Secretary and under the seal of the said Corporation, that the Agreement of Merger to which this certificate is attached, after having been first duly signed in behalf of said Corporation by the President

and Secretary of   , a corporation of the State of
                              , was duly submitted to the shareholders of said
                              , at a special meeting of said shareholders called and
held separately from the meeting of shareholders of any other corporation, upon
waiver of notice, signed by all shareholders, for the purpose of considering and
taking action upon said Agreement of Merger, that shares of stock of said
Corporation were on said date issued and outstanding and that the holders of
        shares voted by ballot in favor of said Agreement of Merger and the holders
of   shares voted by ballot against same, the said affirmative vote representing
at least a majority of the total number of shares of the outstanding capital stock of
said Corporation, and that thereby the Agreement of Merger was at said meeting
duly adopted as the act of the shareholders of said
and the duly adopted agreement of the said Corporation.   ,

     WITNESS my hand and seal of said   on this
    day of   , 19   .

_____
               Secretary

(SEAL)

BOARD OF DIRECTORS' RESOLUTION APPROVING MERGER WITH WHOLLY OWNED SUBSIDIARY

WHEREAS, the Board of Directors of this Corporation has determined that the Corporation now owns all stock of   , a corporation organized under the laws of the State of   , and

WHEREAS, has determined there are efficiencies to be gained by merging   into this Corporation, it is hereby

RESOLVED, that this Corporation hereby merge with   and that this Corporation shall be the Surviving Corporation after the merger is effected and shall assume all of the debts and liabilities of   , and it is

FURTHER RESOLVED, that a special meeting of this Corporation's shareholders shall be called and held for the following purposes: (1) to vote upon the recommendation of the Board of Directors that   be merged into this Corporation, and (2) to approve a merger agreement between   , and this Corporation. The aforementioned shareholders' meeting is to be called and held at the following time, date and place:

[Add Time, Date and Location Clause (see p. 14).]

[Insert Secretary's Certificate #1 (see p. 13).]

(SEAL)

SHAREHOLDERS' RESOLUTION APPROVING MERGER WITH WHOLLY OWNED SUBSIDIARY

WHEREAS, this Corporation is the sole shareholder of

, a corporation that was organized and exists under the authority of the laws of the State of   , and

WHEREAS, the Board of Directors of this Corporation has determined it is advisable that this Company merge with said Corporation in order to obtain operating efficiencies, it is hereby:

RESOLVED, that the shareholders of   hereby approve the adoption of the Agreement of Merger, dated   ,

19   , that was approved on   , 19   by the Board of

Directors of   , and on   , 19   ,

by the Board of Directors of   ; and it is

FURTHER RESOLVED, that a copy of the aforementioned Agreement of Merger shall be attached to the minutes of this meeting.

[Insert Secretary's Certificate #2 (see p. 13).]

(SEAL)

SHAREHOLDERS' RESOLUTION FOR BLANKET AUTHORITY TO SELL CORPORATE PROPERTY

RESOLVED, that the Board of Directors of this Corporation is authorized to sell or exchange all or any part of this Corporation's property and assets, real or personal, tangible or intangible, including goodwill, upon such terms and conditions as the Board of Directors shall determine are in the best interests of the Corporation.

[Insert Secretary's Certificate #2 (see p. 13).]

(SEAL)

BOARD OF DIRECTORS' RESOLUTION OF ACCEPTANCE OFFER TO PURCHASE CORPORATE ASSETS SUBJECT TO SHAREHOLDERS' APPROVAL

WHEREAS, this Corporation has received an offer from
to purchase all of this Corporation's property and assets, real and personal, tangible and intangible, on the terms and conditions set forth in the attached proposal dated   , 19   , and

WHEREAS, in the opinion of this Board of Directors, it is for the best interests of this Corporation to accept the above-described offer, it is hereby

RESOLVED, that the offer of said   , dated
        , 19   and attached to the minutes of this meeting, is hereby accepted, subject to the approval of this Corporation's shareholders, and it is

FURTHER RESOLVED, that the President and the Secretary deliver an acceptance of the above-described offer upon the adoption of a resolution by the Corporation's shareholders authorizing the acceptance the above-described offer, and it is

FURTHER RESOLVED, that the Secretary of this Corporation is hereby directed to call a special meeting of the Corporation's shareholders, to act on this resolution of the Board of Directors, and the Secretary is further directed to give notice that the special meeting of shareholders will be held at the following time, date and location:

[Add Time, Date and Location Clause (see p. 14).]
[Insert Secretary's Certificate #1 (see p. 13).]
(SEAL)

SHAREHOLDERS' RESOLUTION FOR APPROVAL OF
SALE OF CORPORATE ASSETS

RESOLVED, that the shareholders of this Corporation do hereby authorize and approve of the sale of the Corporation's assets to   , on the terms and conditions set out in an Agreement of Sale dated
         , 19   , a copy of which is attached to the minutes of this meeting.

[Insert Secretary's Certificate #2 (see p. 13).]

(SEAL)

CERTIFICATE OF SHAREHOLDERS' CONSENT TO APPROVAL OF SALE OF ALL CORPORATE ASSETS

The undersigned, the holders of all of the shares of stock of the _____ Corporation, hereby consent to the transfer of all of the property of this Corporation to _____ , subject, however, to the agreement of the purchaser to assume all the debts and obligations of this Corporation of every name, type and nature, and upon such other terms as are set out in an Agreement of Sale dated _____ , 19___ , a copy of which is attached to this Consent.

Name of Shareholder	Signature	Number of Shares
_____	_____	_____
_____	_____	_____
_____	_____	_____
_____	_____	_____
_____	_____	_____
_____	_____	_____
_____	_____	_____
_____	_____	_____

_____
Secretary

BOARD OF DIRECTORS' RESOLUTION FOR DISTRIBUTION OF PROCEEDS FROM SALE OF CORPORATE ASSETS

RESOLVED, that the sum of   dollars ($) per share shall be distributed to the shareholders of record of this Corporation as of the   day of   , 19   , as a liquidation payment, and

FURTHER RESOLVED, that the Board of Directors hereby approves of the attached letter, which is to be sent to the shareholders of this Corporation by the President of this Corporation, announcing the liquidation of this Corporation.

[Insert Secretary's Certificate #1 (see p. 13).]

BOARD OF DIRECTORS' RESOLUTION ADVISING DISSOLUTION AND CALLING SHAREHOLDERS' MEETING

Upon a duly made, seconded motion, the following resolution was adopted by the affirmative and unanimous vote of the Board of Directors of

:

RESOLVED, that this Corporation should be dissolved; and it is

FURTHER RESOLVED, that in a manner prescribed by law and by the Bylaws of this Corporation, a special meeting of all shareholders of this Corporation be called to take action upon this resolution and is hereby called, and that such meeting is to be held at the following time, date and place:

[Add Time, Date and Location Clause (see p. 14).]

[Insert Secretary's Certificate #1 (see p. 13).]

(SEAL)

SHAREHOLDERS' RESOLUTION FOR APPROVAL OF DISSOLUTION

Upon a duly made and seconded motion, the following resolution was adopted by the affirmative vote of all of the shareholders of

:

RESOLVED, that   , shall dissolve forthwith, and it is

FURTHER RESOLVED, that the President and Secretary of this Corporation are hereby authorized and directed to file the necessary Certificate of Dissolution of this Corporation in accordance with the laws of the State of

[Insert Secretary's Certificate #2 (see p. 13).]
(SEAL)

CERTIFICATE OF DISSOLUTION

We, the holders of all of the outstanding shares of stock of
_____, entitled to vote on the dissolution of this
Corporation in accordance with Section ____ of the Laws of the State of
_____, do certify:

1. The name of the Corporation is _____ .
2. The Corporation's Articles of Incorporation were accepted for filing and
   filed by the Secretary of State of the State of _____
   on _____ , 19 ____ .
3. The names and addresses the Corporation's Directors are as follows:

   Name   Address

   _____   _____
   _____   _____
   _____   _____
   _____   _____
   _____   _____

4. The names and addresses of the Corporation's officers are as follows:

   Name   Title   Residence

   _____ _____ _____
   _____ _____ _____
   _____ _____ _____
   _____ _____ _____
   _____ _____ _____

5. The Corporation elects to dissolve.
6. The Corporation has only one class of stock.
7. The dissolution of the Corporation was authorized at a special meeting of
   shareholders by _____ vote.

IN WITNESS WHEREOF, we have signed our names to this certificate.

_____
Shareholder

_____
Shareholder

Dated: _____, 19____.

BOARD OF DIRECTORS' RESOLUTION ADVISING FILING OF BANKRUPTCY AND CALLING SHAREHOLDERS' MEETING

WHEREAS, the Board of Directors of this Corporation has determined the Corporation is unable to meet its obligations as they become due in the usual course of business, and,

WHEREAS, the Board of Directors has also determined that the Corporation can no longer continue in business profitably, and,

WHEREAS, the Board of Directors has been advised that various creditors have threatened to prosecute claims against the Corporation, it is hereby

RESOLVED, that, this Corporation file a voluntary petition in bankruptcy, and it is

FURTHER RESOLVED, that a special meeting of the Corporation's shareholders to consider the directors' recommendation that the Corporation file a voluntary petition in bankruptcy, be held at the following time, date and place:

[Add Time, Date and Location Clause (see p. 14).]

And it is

FURTHER RESOLVED, that the Secretary of this Corporation is hereby instructed and directed to send notice to all the Corporation's shareholders of the special meeting of shareholders.

[Insert Secretary's Certificate #1 (see p. 13).]

(SEAL)

CHAPTER 5

Dividends

Regular and Extra Dividends

Form 3000 is the basic standard format for the declaration of a dividend. By acknowledging that a surplus is available, the resolution meets the minimum statutory requirements for the declaration of a dividend. Note that Form 3000 is a resolution for a stock dividend, by replacing the words "stock dividend," with the words "cash dividend," this form can be used when the board wishes to pay a cash dividend. In the alternative, the board may choose to pay a dividend in property. The board may elect to take this course of action when it has property it no longer needs and seeks to pay a dividend.

Form 3010 is a resolution stating the board's dividend policy. The companion Form 3011 can be used to declare a regular dividend in accordance with board policy. Likewise, Form 3012 can be used whenever the board finds it necessary to skip a regular dividend. Form 3013 can be used whenever the board finds it appropriate to declare an extra dividend in addition to the regular dividend.

Dividends Paid with Loan

Where the financial statement shows a capital surplus but the corporation is short of cash to pay a dividend, Form 3020 may be used to authorize a loan to pay the dividend. To create a surplus so that a dividend can be paid, Form 3030 can be used by the board to authorize a reappraisal of assets to allow a transfer of the increased book value of the assets from the property, plant and equipment account to the surplus account. Form 3031 can be used to authorize the transfer and to instruct the accounting firm to adjust the company's financial statements and records accordingly.

Form 3040 is comparable to Forms 3030 and 3031, except that it specifically relates to making an adjustment in the company's reserve for depreciation and to converting the excess reserve to surplus, so that dividends may be paid.

Dissenting from Board Action

If the board of directors votes to declare and pay a dividend when the corporation was not entitled to pay it, then the directors themselves can be held personally liable for the amount of the improper dividend. To avoid liability, a director should take the following steps. First, if the director attends the meeting at which the dividend is declared, he or she should vote against the proposal and demand that the secretary of the corporation register the director's dissent in the minutes of the meeting. If the director did not attend the meeting, then, as soon as he or she becomes aware of that action, the director should send a registered letter to the corporation's secretary demanding that the director's dissent be recorded in the meeting's minutes. Form 3041 provides the format for a dissent.

BOARD OF DIRECTORS' RESOLUTION DECLARING STOCK DIVIDEND

Upon a duly made and seconded motion the following resolution was adopted by the unanimous vote of the Board of Directors of   :

WHEREAS, the financial statement of this Corporation's Treasurer reports that the Corporation has a surplus of   dollars ($) resulting from its business operations for the fiscal year ending on the   day of   , 19   , it is hereby

RESOLVED, that a stock dividend be and hereby is declared in the amount of   dollars ($) per share of the common stock of this Corporation, and that the same shall be paid on   , 19   , to shareholders of record as of   , 19   , and it is

FURTHER RESOLVED, that the Corporation's Treasurer is hereby authorized to transfer   dollars ($) from surplus to the capital account.

[Insert Secretary's Certificate #1 (see p. 13).]

(SEAL)

BOARD OF DIRECTORS' RESOLUTION STATING CORPORATION'S DIVIDEND POLICY

Upon a duly made and seconded motion, the Board of Directors of
unanimously adopted the following resolution:

RESOLVED, that it is this Corporation's dividend policy to pay a dividend
of   dollars ($) per annum on the common stock of the
Corporation, payable in quarterly installments on the first day of   ,
,   and   , if (a) the earnings of the
Corporation support such payments under the laws of the State of
and (b) the Board of Directors determines that the payment of such
dividends is in the best interests of the Corporation.

[Insert Secretary's Certificate #1 (see p. 13).]

(SEAL)

BOARD OF DIRECTORS' RESOLUTION DECLARING A REGULAR DIVIDEND

Upon a duly made, seconded and unanimously carried motion, the following resolution was adopted by the Board of Directors of   :

WHEREAS, the financial statement submitted to the Board of Directors by the Treasurer of this Corporation reveals that there continues to be a surplus resulting from the Corporation's operations since the last quarterly report submitted by the Treasurer on the   day of   , 19   , and that the surplus now amounts to   dollars ($), it is hereby:

RESOLVED, that a portion of the aforementioned surplus, in the amount of   dollars ($), be set aside for the purpose of paying a dividend on the common stock of this Corporation, and the Treasurer is hereby directed to pay a dividend of   dollars ($) per share on all shares of common stock issued and outstanding to those shareholders who were shareholders of record on the   day of   , 19   .

[Insert Secretary's Certificate #1 (see p. 13).]

(SEAL)

BOARD OF DIRECTORS' RESOLUTION SKIPPING A DIVIDEND

Upon a duly made, seconded and unanimously carried motion, the Board of Directors of this Corporation adopted the following resolution:

WHEREAS, it is the concern of the Board of Directors that this Corporation may be required to seek borrowed funds in the next fiscal year and that such a requirement may require the Corporation to present to a borrower a financial statement showing a substantial surplus account, it is hereby

RESOLVED, that a regular dividend will not be declared on the common stock of this Corporation for the   quarter of 19   , and that the amount so saved is to be retained by the Corporation in its surplus account.

[Insert Secretary's Certificate #1 (see p. 13).]

(SEAL)

BOARD OF DIRECTORS' RESOLUTION DECLARING AN EXTRA DIVIDEND

Upon a duly made, seconded and unanimously carried motion, the following resolution was adopted by the Board of Directors of this Corporation:

WHEREAS, the financial statement submitted by the Treasurer of this Corporation to the Board of Directors reveals that the Corporation has a surplus of _____ dollars ($ _____), for the fiscal year ending on the _____ day of _____ , 19____ , it is hereby

RESOLVED, that the regular dividend of _____ dollars ($ _____) per share shall be supplemented by an additional payment of _____ dollars ($ _____) per share so that the total amount of the regular dividend and the extra dividend shall be _____ dollars ($ _____) per share, and the Treasurer is hereby directed to set aside a sufficient portion of the current surplus to satisfy such dividend payment and the Treasurer is further directed to make such dividend payable to all shareholders of record at the close of business on the _____ day of _____ , 19____ .

[Insert Secretary's Certificate #1 (see p. 13).]
(SEAL)

BOARD OF DIRECTORS' RESOLUTION AUTHORIZING LOAN TO PAY DIVIDEND

Upon a duly made, seconded and unanimously carried motion, the Board of Directors of this Corporation adopted the following resolution:

WHEREAS, the financial statement submitted to the Board of Directors of this Corporation reveals that there is a surplus of   dollars ($), which would be sufficient to support the payment of the regular dividend scheduled to be declared at this time, and

WHEREAS, the Corporation's accounts receivable have not been timely paid for the past quarter, and

WHEREAS, the Corporation has obtained a short-term loan, it is hereby

RESOLVED, that regular quarterly dividends shall be declared and paid out of the proceeds of the short-term loan made by the   Bank to all shareholders of record on the   day of   , 19   .

[Insert Secretary's Certificate #1 (see p. 13).]

(SEAL)

BOARD OF DIRECTORS' RESOLUTION AUTHORIZING REAPPRAISAL OF ASSETS

Upon a duly made, seconded and unanimously carried motion, the Board of Directors of this Corporation adopted the following resolution:

WHEREAS, the Board of Directors of this Corporation has been advised by its accountant that the value of the Corporation's assets, both real and personal, tangible and intangible, are reflected at far less than their true market value on the Corporation's books, and

WHEREAS, it is the intent of the Board of Directors to seek debt financing for the Corporation from a lending institution and it is the belief of the Board of Directors that those efforts will be enhanced if the aforementioned assets are carried on the books of the Corporation at a value that reflects their true market value, it is hereby

RESOLVED, that the President of this Corporation is hereby directed to retain the services of an independent firm to appraise the value of the Corporation's assets, both real and personal, tangible and intangible.

[Insert Secretary's Certificate #1 (see p. 13).]

(SEAL)

BOARD OF DIRECTORS' RESOLUTION AUTHORIZING ADJUSTMENT IN SURPLUS AFTER REAPPRAISAL OF ASSETS

Upon a duly made, seconded and unanimously carried motion, the Board of Directors of this Corporation adopted the following resolution:

WHEREAS, this Board directed the President of this Corporation to retain the services of an independent appraisal firm to appraise the assets, both real and personal, tangible and intangible, of this Corporation, and

WHEREAS, the President in fact retained the firm of to perform the appraisal requested by the Board, and

WHEREAS, the firm of   reported that the Corporation's assets as carried on its books have a total value of dollars ($) less than their true market value, it is hereby:

RESOLVED, that the values of the Corporation's various assets as shown in the report by the firm of   , dated   , 19   , a copy of which is attached to the minutes of this meeting, shall be accepted as the value of the Corporation's assets and shall be carried on the Corporation's books at the values shown in that report, and it is

FURTHER RESOLVED, that the Treasurer of the Corporation is hereby directed to make such changes to the books of the Corporation as are necessary for those books to reflect the true market values of the assets of this Corporation as shown in the report of the firm of   .

[Insert Secretary's Certificate #1 (see p. 13).]

(SEAL)

BOARD OF DIRECTORS' RESOLUTION AUTHORIZING CONVERSION OF EXCESS DEPRECIATION TO SURPLUS

Upon a duly made, seconded and unanimously carried motion, the Board of Directors of this Corporation adopted the following resolution:

WHEREAS,   dollars ($) have been assigned to the depreciation account on the Corporation's books for the period running from the

day of   , 19   to the   day of   , 19   , and

WHEREAS,   dollars ($) have been assigned to the reserve for depreciation on the books of the Corporation, and

WHEREAS, the value of the real property upon which the above mentioned depreciation and reserve for depreciation charges and credits were made has been determined by the independent appraisal firm of   to

be   dollars ($), it is hereby

RESOLVED, that the Treasurer of this Corporation is hereby directed to transfer on the Corporation's books   dollars ($) from the Corporation's reserve for buildings account to the Corporation's surplus account.

[Insert Secretary's Certificate #1 (see p. 13).]

(SEAL)

DIRECTOR'S DISSENT—DECLARATION OF DIVIDEND

Date: , 19   .

To: , Secretary,   Corporation

Subject: Dissent from Board Action Declaring Dividend

    I hereby notify you of my dissent from the action taken by the Board of Directors of   Corporation at its meeting of   , 19   , at which the Board voted to declare and pay a dividend of   dollars ($) per share to all shareholders of record on   , 19   .

    As the minutes of that meeting should reflect, I did not attend that meeting. It is my opinion that the dividend authorized by the Board at the aforesaid   , 19   , meeting is illegal because there is no surplus to support the payment.

    I hereby demand that you enter my dissent in the minutes of the meeting of   , 19   , from the Board's action authorizing the aforementioned dividend and that you advise each member of the Board of this demand.

Sincerely,

_____

Director,   Corporation

CHAPTER **6**

Compensation

Salary

Form 4000 is a standard board resolution for changing officers' salaries. The minutes of the meeting at which this resolution is adopted should reflect whatever factors and documents the board considered in deciding that the salary granted to each officer is reasonable. It can be used for any officer.

Form 4010 is the board resolution calling for officers to repay any part of their salary that is declared to be unreasonable and nondeductible by the IRS or a court. Form 4011 may be filled out and signed by each officer, and it is the officers' binding commitment to repay the excessive portion of their salary.

Form 4020 is a board resolution terminating until further notice the salaries of the corporation's officers.

Bonuses

The board of directors has wide discretion in granting bonuses to employees. A bonus can be given to just one employee or to every employee. It can be a stated amount or a percentage of profits. It can be in stock or an option on stock. It can be a token to honor a particular employee or a particular occasion, such as Christmas. In any case, the main concern of the board should be to make sure that the bonus is reasonable. The minutes of the board meeting should show why the board finds the bonus amount to be reasonable. It is also helpful to state the reasons for the bonus in the "Whereas" clauses of the resolution authorizing the bonus.

Form 4100 is a board resolution to grant officers a bonus based on a percentage of the company's net profits.

Form 4110 is a resolution granting a bonus of a specific amount to each officer.

Form 4120 is a resolution granting officers a bonus in the form of the company's stock.

Form 4130 is a resolution granting an option to purchase shares of the company's stock. This resolution is a one-time affair and should not be confused with Form 6200, which sets up a continuing stock option plan.

Form 4140 is a board resolution authorizing payment of an honorarium to an employee in recognition of special services.

Form 4150 is a resolution granting a holiday bonus to all employees on the basis of a percentage of each employee's salary.

Fees

Directors who are also officers generally receive no special fee for attending board meetings, as such matters are assumed to be covered by their salary and other compensation. Nonsalaried directors, however, may be granted a fee for attending board meetings, in addition to the expense allowance that all directors may be entitled to receive. Form 4160 is a resolution the board may use to set the fee of nonsalaried directors.

BOARD OF DIRECTORS' RESOLUTION CHANGING OFFICERS' SALARIES

Upon a duly made, seconded and unanimously carried motion, the Board of Directors of this Corporation adopted the following resolution:

RESOLVED, that the annual salaries of the officers of this Corporation for the one-year period beginning on the   day of   , 19   and ending on the   day of   , 19   , shall be as follows:

President: dollars ($)

Vice President: dollars ($)

Secretary: dollars ($)

Treasurer: dollars ($)

And it is

FURTHER RESOLVED, that the above-mentioned salaries shall be payable in equal installments every   .

[Insert Secretary's Certificate #1 (see p. 13).]

(SEAL)

BOARD OF DIRECTORS' RESOLUTION CALLING FOR REPAYMENT OF SALARY DECLARED UNREASONABLE

Upon a duly made, seconded and unanimously carried motion, the Board of Directors of this Corporation adopted the following resolution:

RESOLVED, that in the event any portion of an officer's salary will be disallowed by the Internal Revenue Service of the Department of the Treasury of the United States as unreasonable in amount, such officer or officers shall be required to pay to this Corporation the full amount that will be disallowed by the Internal Revenue Service as unreasonable compensation.

[Insert Secretary's Certificate #1 (see p. 13).]

(SEAL)

OFFICERS' CONSENT FOR REPAYMENT OF COMPENSATION DECLARED UNREASONABLE

The undersigned, each an officer of the

Corporation, agrees that in the event that any part of my compensation will be disallowed by the Internal Revenue Service of the Department of the Treasury of the United States as unreasonable compensation and an unreasonable deduction in the calculation of this Corporation's federal income tax liability I shall repay to the Corporation within   days after a final disallowance of such deduction by the Internal Revenue Service and the conclusion of any appeals I may choose to make from such a determination.

Name	Title	Signature

BOARD OF DIRECTORS' RESOLUTION TERMINATING OFFICERS' SALARIES

Upon a duly made, seconded and unanimously carried motion, the Board of Directors of this Corporation adopted the following resolution:

RESOLVED, notwithstanding any previously adopted resolution to the contrary, effective immediately the following officers of the Corporation shall serve without any compensation whatsoever: ,

                    ,   and
          .

[Insert Secretary's Certificate #1 (see p. 13).]
(SEAL)

BOARD OF DIRECTORS' RESOLUTION SETTING OFFICERS' BONUS BASED ON NET PROFITS

Upon a duly made, seconded and unanimously carried motion, the Board of Directors of this Corporation adopted the following resolution:

WHEREAS   , the President of this Corporation, has surpassed the highest expectation of the Board of Directors by obtaining for the Corporation   contracts for the sale of   , said contracts totaling   dollars ($) in new orders, it is hereby

RESOLVED, that   , the President of this Corporation, shall be compensated for his/her outstanding service by payment of a commission of   percent of all contracts procured by him/her, with said commission to be calculated on the following annual basis, starting with the

       day of   , 19   : no commission shall be paid for the first   dollars ($) in contract business procured for the Corporation by   ; on all contract business procured by the President above   dollars ($), he/she shall be entitled to a commission of   percent of the dollar value of each such contract.

   [Insert Secretary's Certificate #1 (see p. 13).]

   (SEAL)

BOARD OF DIRECTORS' RESOLUTION SETTING OFFICERS' BONUS AT A STATED AMOUNT

Upon a duly made, seconded and unanimously carried motion, the Board of Directors of this Corporation adopted the following resolution:

WHEREAS, the Board of Directors' Compensation Committee has submitted recommendations with respect to year-end bonuses to be paid to the officers of this Corporation, and

WHEREAS, the Corporation's operations have exceeded the expectations of the Board at the beginning of this fiscal year, it is hereby

RESOLVED, that the Board of Directors do and hereby does adopt the Compensation Committee's recommendations contained in its report to the Board dated _____ , 19 ___ , a copy of which is attached to these minutes, and accordingly year-end bonuses shall be paid to the following officers:

Officer   Amount

_____   _____

_____   _____

_____   _____

And it is

FURTHER RESOLVED, that the Treasurer is hereby directed to make the above-described bonus payments to the officers listed above on the ___ day of _____ , 19 ___ .

[Insert Secretary's Certificate #1 (see p. 13).]

(SEAL)

BOARD OF DIRECTORS' RESOLUTION FOR OFFICERS' BONUS TO BE PAID IN STOCK

Upon a duly made, seconded and unanimously adopted motion, the Board of Directors of this Corporation adopted the following resolution:

WHEREAS, the Compensation Committee of the Board of Directors has presented the Board with its recommendations regarding the possibility of providing the officers of this Corporation with additional compensation in the form of a stock bonus, it is hereby

RESOLVED, that the recommendation of the Compensation Committee in its report dated _____ , 19 ___ , a copy of which is attached to the minutes of this meeting, be and hereby is adopted, and the Treasurer of this Corporation is hereby directed to issue to the following officers the number of shares of common stock set out after their names:

Officer   Number of Shares

_____   _____

_____   _____

_____   _____

_____   _____

_____   _____

[Insert Secretary's Certificate #1 (see p. 13).]
(SEAL)

BOARD OF DIRECTORS' RESOLUTION FOR OFFICERS' BONUS TO BE PAID AS A STOCK OPTION

Upon a duly made, seconded and unanimously adopted motion, the Board of Directors of this Corporation adopted the following resolution:

WHEREAS, the Compensation Committee of the Board of Directors has presented the Board with its recommendations regarding the possibility of providing the President of this Corporation with additional compensation in the form of a stock option, it is hereby

RESOLVED, that the recommendation of the Compensation Committee in its report dated   , 19   , a copy of which is attached to the minutes of this meeting, be and hereby is adopted, and,   , the President of this Corporation, is hereby advised that in return for the payment of   dollars ($) on or before the   day of   , 19   , he/she will receive an option to purchase   shares of the common stock of this Corporation at any time before the   day of   , 19   , in return for the payment of   dollars ($) per share, and it is

FURTHER RESOLVED, that the Corporation's Treasurer is hereby directed to retain in the Corporation's Treasury a sufficient number of shares of the Corporation's common stock to satisfy the above-described option.

[Insert Secretary's Certificate #1 (see p. 13).]

(SEAL)

BOARD OF DIRECTORS' RESOLUTION FOR HONORARIUM FOR SPECIAL SERVICE

Upon a duly made, seconded and unanimously adopted motion, the Board of Directors of this Corporation adopted the following resolution:

WHEREAS, the Compensation Committee appointed by this Board of Directors has presented the Board with its recommendations regarding the performance of   , the   of this Corporation, suggesting that the aforesaid individual be rewarded with an honorarium for extraordinary services unrelated to his/her duties as the   of this Corporation, it is hereby

RESOLVED, that the recommendation of the Compensation Committee in its report dated   , 19   , a copy of which the Secretary of the Corporation is directed to attach to the minutes of this meeting, be and hereby is adopted, and the Treasurer of this Corporation is hereby directed to pay the sum of   dollars ($) to the aforementioned   , on or before the   day of   , 19   .

[Insert Secretary's Certificate #1 (see p. 13).]

(SEAL)

BOARD OF DIRECTORS' RESOLUTION SETTING HOLIDAY BONUS FOR EMPLOYEES

Upon a duly made, seconded and unanimously adopted motion, the Board of Directors of this Corporation adopted the following resolution:

WHEREAS, the Compensation Committee has presented the Board with its recommendations concerning the possibility of providing the employees of this Corporation with additional compensation in the form of a holiday cash bonus, it is hereby

RESOLVED, that the recommendation of the Compensation Committee in its report dated   , 19   , copy of which is attached to the minutes of this meeting, be and hereby is adopted, and the Treasurer is hereby directed to pay a cash holiday bonus to employees of this Corporation on the day of   , 19   , according to the following formula:

1. Every employee employed for less than   months shall receive a cash bonus equal to his or her ordinary salary for   week(s);
2. Every employee employed for longer than   months and less than   months shall receive a cash bonus equal to his or her ordinary salary for   weeks;
3. Every employee employed for longer than   months shall receive a cash bonus equal to his or her ordinary salary for   weeks.

[Insert Secretary's Certificate #1 (see p. 13).]
(SEAL)

BOARD OF DIRECTORS' RESOLUTION FIXING ATTENDANCE FEES FOR DIRECTORS

Upon a duly made, seconded and unanimously adopted motion, the Board of Directors of this Corporation adopted the following resolution:

WHEREAS, the Compensation Committee appointed by this Board of Directors has presented the Board with its recommendations regarding the Board's inquiry concerning the possibility of providing the directors of this Corporation with compensation for their attendance at regular and special meetings of the Board of Directors, it is hereby

RESOLVED, that the recommendation of the Compensation Committee in its report dated   , 19   , a copy of which the Secretary of the Corporation is directed to attach to the minutes of this meeting, be and hereby is adopted, and the Treasurer of this Corporation is hereby directed to pay to each director who attends a regular or special meeting of this Corporation's Board of Directors the sum of   dollars ($) per meeting, effective with the next regular or special meeting of the Board of Directors following this meeting.

[Insert Secretary's Certificate #1 (see p. 13).]

(SEAL)

CHAPTER 7

Fringe Benefits

Expense Accounts

Form 5000 is a resolution authorizing the president to charge to the company any expenses incidental to carrying on the company's business. If the board wishes to extend this privilege to other officers or employees, it can use Form 5000 and substitute the appropriate names and titles for the president.

Form 5001 is a board resolution authorizing the corporation to reimburse the president for expenses incurred in connection with the corporation's business. Again, this form can be easily adapted to provide reimbursement for other officers and employees.

Form 5010 is a board resolution authorizing the corporation to purchase a country club membership on behalf of a corporate officer for use in connection with the corporation's business. Note that under current tax laws country club memberships may not be a deductible expense.

Loans

Form 5030 is a board resolution authorizing a loan to a corporate officer or employee. Form 5031 is a shareholder resolution approving a loan to a corporate officer or employee.

For the most part, loans to officers—even interest-free loans—can be made if it is in the interest of the corporation to do so. Loans to directors are not permitted in most states unless the director is also an officer of the corporation. If a loan is made to a director or officer when it is improper to do so, board members should dissent from the action in order to avoid personal liability on the loan. The dissent should be made at the meeting at which the loan was authorized, and the dissenting director should demand that the secretary place the director's dissent on the record. If the director did not attend the meeting at which an improper loan was authorized, then as soon as the director becomes aware of the board's action, he or she should immediately send a registered letter to the secretary of the corporation dissenting from the board's action.

Death Benefit Contract

Form 5040 authorizes the corporation to purchase a death benefit contract for an officer. This resolution is tailored to the tax provision allowing corporations to purchase up to $5,000 of such insurance. The premiums are deductible by the corporation and tax-free to the covered individual.

BOARD OF DIRECTORS' RESOLUTION AUTHORIZING PRESIDENT'S EXPENSE ACCOUNT

Upon a duly made, seconded and unanimously adopted motion, the Board of Directors of this Corporation adopted the following resolution:

WHEREAS, the Board of Directors has determined that the duties of the President of this Corporation now require him/her to travel to various locations and to entertain prospective clients on a regular basis, it is hereby

RESOLVED, that   , the President of this Corporation, is hereby authorized to open a credit card charge account in the name of this Corporation with the   finance company and to list himself/herself as an authorized user of the credit card issued in connection with the credit card charge account and to charge to that account all expenses the President will incur in the Corporation's behalf related to travel and/or entertainment.

[Insert Secretary's Certificate #1 (see p. 13).]
(SEAL)

BOARD OF DIRECTORS' RESOLUTION AUTHORIZING REIMBURSEMENT TO OFFICER

Upon a duly made, seconded and unanimously adopted motion, the Board of Directors of this Corporation adopted the following resolution:

WHEREAS, the Treasurer of this Corporation, in a memorandum dated   , 19   , a copy of which is attached to the minutes of this meeting, has reported to the Board of Directors that   , the President of the Corporation, has incurred expenses in connection with   , it is hereby

RESOLVED, that this Corporation reimburse the President of this Corporation for the expenses incurred by the President and described in the report of the Treasurer dated   , 19   , a copy of which the Secretary of the Corporation is directed to attach to the minutes of this meeting, and the Treasurer is hereby directed to make such payment to the President forthwith.

[Insert Secretary's Certificate #1 (see p. 13).]

(SEAL)

BOARD OF DIRECTORS' RESOLUTION AUTHORIZING PURCHASE OF COUNTRY CLUB MEMBERSHIP

Upon a duly made, seconded and unanimously adopted motion, the Board of Directors of this Corporation adopted the following resolution:

WHEREAS, this Board of Directors has before it a report from the Corporation's President, dated   , 19   , concerning the benefits that would flow to this Corporation if its President could entertain at a private club potential and existing customers, and

WHEREAS, membership in such private clubs is limited to individuals and is not open to businesses, it is hereby

RESOLVED, that the recommendation of the President in his or her report dated   , 19   , a copy of which is attached to the minutes of this meeting, be and hereby is adopted, and the President of this Corporation is hereby authorized to apply for membership in the   Club, in his or her own name, and it is

FURTHER RESOLVED, that the Treasurer of this Corporation is hereby directed to reimburse the President for any and all expenses he or she has incurred and will incur at the   Club on behalf of this Corporation.

[Insert Secretary's Certificate #1 (see p. 13).]
(SEAL)

BOARD OF DIRECTORS' RESOLUTION AUTHORIZING LOANS TO DIRECTORS, OFFICERS OR EMPLOYEES

Upon a duly made, seconded and unanimously adopted motion, the Board of Directors of this Corporation adopted the following resolution:

WHEREAS, the President of this Corporation has presented the Board with a recommendation that the Board of Directors approve a loan to

_____, the _____ of this Corporation, and

WHEREAS, the aforementioned _____ has been a valued officer of this Corporation for the past _____, and the Board believes it is in the best interests of the Corporation to assist _____ in this time of financial difficulties, it is hereby

RESOLVED, that the recommendation of the Corporation's President in his/her report dated _____, 19___, a copy of which is attached to the minutes of this meeting, be and hereby is adopted, and the Treasurer of this Corporation is hereby directed to lend, on the behalf of the Corporation,

_____ dollars ($_____) to _____ on the following terms and conditions:

[Insert Secretary's Certificate #1 (see p. 13).]
(SEAL)

SHAREHOLDERS' RESOLUTION APPROVING LOANS TO DIRECTORS, OFFICERS OR EMPLOYEES

Upon a duly made, seconded and unanimously adopted motion, the shareholders of this Corporation adopted the following resolution:

WHEREAS, the Board of Directors has presented the shareholders with its resolution recommending that this Corporation provide ,
                                of this Corporation, with a loan in the amount of
                dollars ($), it is hereby

RESOLVED, that the aforesaid resolution of the Board of Directors, dated
                , 19   , a copy of which the Secretary of the Corporation is directed to attach to the minutes of this meeting, be and hereby is approved, and the Treasurer of this Corporation is hereby directed forthwith to make the aforementioned loan to   on the terms and conditions set out in the above-cited resolution of the Board of Directors.

[Insert Secretary's Certificate #2 (see p. 13).]
(SEAL)

BOARD OF DIRECTORS' RESOLUTION AUTHORIZING PURCHASE OF DEATH BENEFIT CONTRACT

Upon a duly made, seconded and unanimously adopted motion, the Board of Directors of this Corporation adopted the following resolution:

WHEREAS, the Compensation Committee appointed by this Board of Directors has presented the Board with its recommendation that the Board authorizes the creation of a death benefit for employees and officers who have been in the employ of the Corporation for at least   years, it is hereby:

RESOLVED, that the recommendation of the Compensation Committee in its report dated   , 19   , a copy of which the Secretary of the Corporation is directed to attach to the minutes of this meeting, be and hereby is adopted, and the President of this Corporation is hereby directed to advise employees, in writing, that a death benefit in the amount of dollars ($) will be paid to the estate of every employee who (1) is employed by the Corporation at the time of his or her death and (2) at the time of his or her death (a) had been employed by the Corporation for at least the previous   years or (b) had retired and was receiving benefits under the Corporation's retirement program.

[Insert Secretary's Certificate #1 (see p. 13).]

(SEAL)

CHAPTER 8

Employee Benefit Plans

Shareholder Resolutions

Setting up an employee benefit plan entails a long-term commitment of company resources and, for this reason alone, it is sound practice to obtain the approval of the shareholders. Although most plans involve a relatively modest expense, some stock option, pension and profit-sharing plans may require the commitment of significantly greater funds. In these cases, it is prudent to have the shareholders specifically consent to setting aside a certain amount of stock or a percentage of profits to fund these plans.

Form 6000 is a general purpose shareholders' resolution that can be used to obtain approval for almost any employee benefit plan. Form 6100 is a shareholders' resolution to set aside a percentage of profits to fund pension and profit-sharing plans. Form 6110 is a shareholders' resolution for the adoption of a profit-sharing plan, and Form 6120 is for adoption of a pension plan. Form 6200 is a shareholders' resolution to set aside stock for issuance under a stock option plan. Form 6210 is a board resolution to execute the shareholders' resolution on Form 6200.

Plans Providing Future Benefits

These plans offer employees the benefit of having the company pay directly or through an insurer some of their current expenses, such as those for medical and dental expenses (Form 6300), sick pay under a wage continuation plan (Form 6310), group life insurance (Form 6320), split-dollar life insurance (Form 6330), an educational loan program (Form 6340), a scholarship aid program (Form 6350), group legal services (Form 6360) and personal financial counseling services (Form 6370). Here, too, the standard procedure is to attach a copy of the plan to the resolution and insert a copy in the book of minutes.

Because federal law gives employees immediate, long-term rights in employee benefit plans, extreme care should be taken in the selection and adoption of such plans. Banks and insurance companies may be able to offer some assistance, especially with pension and profit-sharing plans, which they often administer on behalf of the corporation.

SHAREHOLDERS' RESOLUTION ADOPTING
EMPLOYEES' WELFARE PLAN

Upon a duly made, seconded and unanimously adopted motion, the shareholders of this Corporation adopted the following resolution:

WHEREAS, the Board of Directors has approved its Compensation Committee's detailed recommendation, the "Welfare Plan for Employees," that the Corporation establish a welfare plan for its employees, it is hereby

RESOLVED, that the "Welfare Plan for Employees of the _____ Corporation" recommended by the Compensation Committee in its report dated _____ , 19___ , a copy of which is attached to the minutes of this meeting, and approved by the Board of Directors at its meeting of _____ , 19___ , the minutes of which are attached to the minutes of this meeting, be and hereby is adopted, and the directors of this Corporation are hereby authorized to take all actions necessary to bring the aforementioned "Welfare Plan for the Employees of _____ Corporation" into being.

[Insert Secretary's Certificate #2 (see p. 13).]
(SEAL)

SHAREHOLDERS' RESOLUTION FOR APPROVAL OF BENEFIT PLAN

Upon a duly made, seconded and unanimously adopted motion, the shareholders of this Corporation adopted the following resolution:

WHEREAS, the Board of Directors of this Corporation has adopted a resolution authorizing the establishment of an Employee Pension and Profit-Sharing Plan, and

WHEREAS, the resolution of the Board of Directors establishing the aforementioned Pension and Profit-Sharing Plan also contains the Board's conclusions on how that Plan shall be funded, it is hereby

RESOLVED, that the Employee Pension and Profit-Sharing Plan approved by the Board of Directors in its resolution dated   , 19   , a copy of which is attached to the minutes of this meeting, be and hereby is adopted; and it is

FURTHER RESOLVED, that the funding for the above mentioned Employee Pension and Profit-Sharing Plan approved by the Board in the aforementioned resolution be and hereby is adopted; and it is

FURTHER RESOLVED, that the Treasurer of this Corporation is hereby directed to set aside from the Corporation's annual net profits a sum not to exceed   percent of the aforesaid net profits to fund the aforementioned Employee Pension and Profit-Sharing Plan and to do everything else necessary to fund the Employee Pension and Profit-Sharing Plan as required by the aforementioned recommendations of the Compensation Committee that were approved by the aforementioned resolution of the Board of Directors.

[Insert Secretary's Certificate #2 (see p. 13).]

(SEAL)

SHAREHOLDERS' RESOLUTION FOR ADOPTION OF PROFIT-SHARING PLAN

Upon a duly made, seconded and unanimously adopted motion, the shareholders of this Corporation adopted the following resolution:

WHEREAS, the Board of Directors of this Corporation has adopted a resolution authorizing the establishment of an Employee Profit-Sharing Plan, it is hereby

RESOLVED, that the Employee Profit-Sharing Plan approved by the Board of Directors in its resolution dated   , 19   , a copy of which the Secretary of the Corporation is directed to attach to the minutes of this meeting, be and hereby is adopted.

[Insert Secretary's Certificate #2 (see p. 13).]

(SEAL)

SHAREHOLDERS' RESOLUTION FOR ADOPTION
OF PENSION PLAN

Upon a duly made, seconded and unanimously adopted motion, the shareholders of this Corporation adopted the following resolution:

WHEREAS, the Board of Directors of this Corporation has adopted a resolution authorizing the establishment of an Employee Pension Plan, it is hereby:

RESOLVED, that the Employee Pension Plan approved by the Board of Directors in its resolution dated   , 19   , a copy of which the Secretary of the Corporation is directed to attach to the minutes of this meeting, be and hereby is adopted.

[Insert Secretary's Certificate #2 (see p. 13).]

(SEAL)

SHAREHOLDERS' RESOLUTION FOR APPROVAL OF STOCK OPTION PLAN

Upon a duly made, seconded and unanimously adopted motion, the shareholders of this Corporation adopted the following resolution:

WHEREAS, the Board of Directors of this Corporation has adopted a resolution authorizing the establishment of a Stock Option Plan, and

WHEREAS, the resolution of the Board of Directors establishing the aforementioned Stock Option Plan also requires the Corporation to have available shares of stock to satisfy the exercise of options under the Plan, it is hereby

RESOLVED, that the Stock Option Plan approved by the Board of Directors in its resolution dated   , 19   , a copy of which the Secretary of the Corporation is directed to attach to the minutes of this meeting, be and hereby is adopted; and it is

FURTHER RESOLVED, that the Treasurer is hereby authorized to set aside in the Corporation's Treasury, as recommended by the Board of Directors in its aforesaid resolution,   shares of the common stock of this Corporation for sale to individuals entitled to exercise an option to purchase such shares under the Stock Option Plan.

[Insert Secretary's Certificate #2 (see p. 13).]

(SEAL)

BOARD OF DIRECTORS' RESOLUTION FOR SETTING ASIDE SHARES OF STOCK FOR A STOCK OPTION PLAN

Upon a duly made, seconded and unanimously adopted motion, the directors of this Corporation adopted the following resolution:

WHEREAS, the shareholders of this Corporation have adopted a resolution, a copy of which is attached to the minutes of this meeting, authorizing the establishment of a Stock Option Plan; and

WHEREAS the resolution of the shareholders establishing the aforementioned Stock Option Plan also requires that the Board of Directors set aside enough shares of the common stock of this Corporation to satisfy the exercise of options under the Plan; it is hereby

RESOLVED, that this Corporation shall set aside   shares of its common stock for the sole purpose of satisfying the exercise of options under the Stock Option Plan.

[Insert Secretary's Certificate #1 (see p. 13).]

(SEAL)

BOARD OF DIRECTORS' RESOLUTION AUTHORIZING ADOPTION OF EMPLOYEE MEDICAL-DENTAL PLAN

Upon a duly made, seconded and unanimously adopted motion, the Board of Directors of this Corporation adopted the following resolution:

WHEREAS, the Board of Directors' Compensation Committee has made a written recommendation that this Corporation establish a health care program providing both medical and dental benefits, and

WHEREAS, the Board of Directors concludes that the establishment of such a program would enable the Corporation to attract and retain desirable employees, it is hereby

RESOLVED, that the Employee Health Plan recommended by the Compensation Committee, a copy of which is attached to the minutes of this meeting, be and hereby is approved, adopted and accepted by the Board of Directors.

[Insert Secretary's Certificate #1 (see p. 13).]
(SEAL)

BOARD OF DIRECTORS' RESOLUTION AUTHORIZING
ADOPTION OF WAGE CONTINUATION PLAN

Upon a duly made, seconded and unanimously adopted motion, the Board of Directors of this Corporation adopted the following resolution:

WHEREAS, the Board of Directors' Compensation Committee has made a written recommendation that the Corporation establish a Wage Continuation Program under which employees who shall become sick, injured or otherwise incapacitated for medical reasons may continue to receive wages, and

WHEREAS, the Board of Directors concludes that the establishment of such a program would enable the Corporation to attract and retain highly qualified, desirable employees, it is hereby

RESOLVED, that the Wage Continuation Plan recommended by the Compensation Committee, a copy of which the Secretary is directed to attach to the minutes of this meeting, be and hereby is approved, adopted and accepted by the Board of Directors of this Corporation effective for all claims made on or after

, 19   .

[Insert Secretary's Certificate #1 (see p. 13).]

(SEAL)

BOARD OF DIRECTORS' RESOLUTION AUTHORIZING ADOPTION OF GROUP LIFE INSURANCE PLAN

Upon a duly made, seconded and unanimously adopted motion, the Board of Directors of this Corporation adopted the following resolution:

WHEREAS, the Compensation Committee of the Board of Directors of this Corporation made a written recommendation that the Corporation establish a group life insurance program for the Corporation's employees, and

WHEREAS, the Board of Directors concludes that the establishment of such a program would enable the Corporation to attract and retain highly qualified, desirable employees, it is hereby

RESOLVED, that the Group Life Insurance Plan recommended by the Compensation Committee, a copy of which the Secretary is directed to attach to the minutes of this meeting, be and hereby is approved, adopted and accepted by the Board of Directors of this Corporation, and it is

FURTHER RESOLVED, that the President of this Corporation is hereby directed to take the necessary measures to execute and bring into being the Group Life Insurance Policy recommended by the Compensation Committee and adopted herein by the Board of Directors.

[Insert Secretary's Certificate #1 (see p. 13).]

(SEAL)

BOARD OF DIRECTORS' RESOLUTION AUTHORIZING
SPLIT-DOLLAR INSURANCE PLAN

Upon a duly made, seconded and unanimously adopted motion, the Board of Directors of this Corporation adopted the following resolution:

WHEREAS, the Compensation Committee of the Board of Directors of this Corporation has made a written recommendation that the Corporation establish a Split-Dollar Insurance Program, and

WHEREAS, the Board of Directors concludes that the establishment of such a program would enable the Corporation to attract and retain highly qualified, desirable employees, it is hereby

RESOLVED, that the Split-Dollar Insurance Program recommended by the Executive Committee, a copy of which the Secretary is directed to attach to the minutes of this meeting, be and hereby is approved, adopted and accepted by the Board of Directors of this Corporation, and it is

FURTHER RESOLVED, that the President of this Corporation is hereby directed to do everything necessary to execute an agreement and bring into existence the Split-Dollar Insurance Program, a copy of which is appended to the minutes of this meeting.

[Insert Secretary's Certificate #1 (see p. 13).]

(SEAL)

BOARD OF DIRECTORS' RESOLUTION AUTHORIZING EDUCATIONAL LOAN PLAN

Upon a duly made, seconded and unanimously adopted motion, the Board of Directors of this Corporation adopted the following resolution:

WHEREAS, the Board of Directors' Compensation Committee has made a written recommendation that the Corporation establish an educational loan plan under which employees would, if they will so desire, receive financial assistance from the Corporation for the purpose of financing the education of their children, and

WHEREAS, the Board of Directors concludes that the establishment of such a program would enable the Corporation to attract and retain highly qualified, desirable employees, it is hereby

RESOLVED, that the "Educational Loan Assistance Plan for the Benefit of the Children of the Employees of   Corporation," recommended by the Compensation Committee, a copy of which is attached to the minutes of this meeting, be and hereby is approved, adopted and accepted by the Board of Directors, and it is

FURTHER RESOLVED, that the President of this Corporation is hereby directed to take all steps necessary to bring the aforesaid Plan into existence.

[Insert Secretary's Certificate #1 (see p. 13).]

(SEAL)

BOARD OF DIRECTORS' RESOLUTION AUTHORIZING SCHOLARSHIP AID PROGRAM

Upon a duly made, seconded and unanimously adopted motion, the Board of Directors of this Corporation adopted the following resolution:

WHEREAS, the Compensation Committee of the Board of Directors of this Corporation has made a written recommendation that the Corporation establish an educational assistance program under which the children of employees could receive educational scholarships from this Corporation, and

WHEREAS, the Board of Directors concludes that the establishment of such a program would enable the Corporation to attract and retain highly qualified, desirable employees, it is hereby

RESOLVED, that the "Scholarship Aid Plan for the Benefit of the Children of the Employees of _____ Corporation," recommended by the Compensation Committee, a copy of which is attached to the minutes of this meeting, be and hereby is approved, adopted and accepted by the Directors of this Corporation, and it is

FURTHER RESOLVED, that the President of this Corporation is hereby directed to take all steps necessary to bring the aforesaid Plan into existence.

[Insert Secretary's Certificate #1 (see p. 13).]

(SEAL)

BOARD OF DIRECTORS' RESOLUTION AUTHORIZING ADOPTION OF GROUP LEGAL SERVICES PLAN

Upon a duly made, seconded and unanimously adopted motion, the Board of Directors of this Corporation adopted the following resolution:

WHEREAS, the Compensation Committee of the Board of Directors of this Corporation has made a written recommendation that the Corporation establish a Group Legal Services Plan under which employees would, if they will so desire, have access to qualified legal counsel without cost to themselves, and

WHEREAS, the Board of Directors concludes that the establishment of such a program would enable the Corporation to attract and retain highly qualified, desirable employees, it is hereby

RESOLVED, that the "Group Legal Assistance Plan for the Benefit of the Employees of   Corporation," recommended by the Compensation Committee, a copy of which the Secretary is directed to attach to the minutes of this meeting, be and hereby is approved, adopted and accepted by the Board of Directors of this Corporation, and it is

FURTHER RESOLVED, that the President of this Corporation is hereby directed to take all steps necessary to bring the aforesaid Plan into existence.

[Insert Secretary's Certificate #1 (see p. 13).]
(SEAL)

BOARD OF DIRECTORS' RESOLUTION AUTHORIZING ADOPTION OF FINANCIAL COUNSELING PLAN

Upon a duly made, seconded and unanimously adopted motion, the Board of Directors of this Corporation adopted the following resolution:

WHEREAS, the Compensation Committee of the Board of Directors of this Corporation has made a written recommendation that the Corporation establish a plan under which employees could obtain financial counseling services without costs to themselves, and

WHEREAS, the Board of Directors concludes that the establishment of such a program would enable the Corporation to attract and retain highly qualified, desirable employees, it is hereby

RESOLVED, that the "Financial Counseling Service Plan for the Benefit of the Employees of _____ Corporation," recommended by the Compensation Committee, a copy of which the Secretary is directed to attach to the minutes of this meeting, be and hereby is approved, adopted and accepted by the Board of Directors of this Corporation, and it is

FURTHER RESOLVED, that the Corporation's President is directed to take all steps necessary to bring the aforesaid Plan into existence.

[Insert Secretary's Certificate #1 (see p. 13).]

(SEAL)

Index

About the Author

Ted Nicholas is a multifaceted business personality. In addition to being a well-known author and respected speaker, Mr. Nicholas remains an active participant in his own entrepreneurial ventures. Without capital, he started his first business at age 21. Since then, he has started 22 companies of his own.

Mr. Nicholas has written 13 books on business and finance since his writing career began in 1972. The best known is *How To Form Your Own Corporation Without a Lawyer for under $75*. His previous business enterprises include Enterprise Publishing, Inc., The Company Corporation and Peterson's House of Fudge, a candy and ice cream manufacturing business conducted through 30 retail stores, as well as other businesses in franchising, real estate, machinery and food.

When the author was only 29, he was selected by a group of business leaders as one of the most outstanding businessmen in the nation and was invited to the White House to meet the President.

Although Mr. Nicholas has founded many successful enterprises, he also has experienced two major setbacks and many minor ones. He considers business setbacks necessary to success and the only true way to learn anything in life, a lesson that goes all the way back to childhood. That's why he teaches other entrepreneurs how to "fail forward."

Mr. Nicholas has appeared on numerous television and radio shows and conducts business seminars in Florida, Switzerland, the UK, Germany and France. Presently, he owns and operates four corporations of his own and acts as marketing consultant and copywriter to small as well as large businesses.

If you have any questions, thoughts or comments, Mr. Nicholas loves to hear from his readers! You are welcome to call, write or fax him at the following address:

P.O. Box 877
Indian Rocks Beach, FL 34635
Phone: 813-596-4966
Fax: 813-596-6900

LICENSE AGREEMENT

OPENING ENVELOPE VOIDS RETURNABILITY OR MONEY-BACK GUARANTEES
PLEASE READ THIS DOCUMENT CAREFULLY BEFORE BREAKING THIS SEAL

By breaking this sealed envelope, you agree to become bound by the terms of this license. If you do not agree to the terms of this license do not use the software and promptly return the unopened package within thirty (30) days to the place where you obtained it for a refund.

This Software is licensed, not sold to you by DEARBORN FINANCIAL PUBLISHING, INC. owner of the product for use only under the terms of this License, and DEARBORN FINANCIAL PUBLISHING, INC. reserves any rights not expressly granted to you.

1. **LICENSE**: This License allows you to:

(a) Use the Software only on a single microcomputer at a time, except the Software may be executed from a common disk shared by multiple CPU's provided that one authorized copy of the Software has been licensed from DEARBORN FINANCIAL PUBLISHING, INC. for each CPU executing the Software. DEARBORN FINANCIAL PUBLISHING, INC. does not, however, guarantee that the Software will function properly in your multiple CPU, multi-user environment. The Software may not be used with any gateways, bridges, modems, and/or network extenders that allow the software to be used on multiple CPU's unless one authorized copy of the Software has been licensed from DEARBORN FINANCIAL PUBLISHING, INC. for each CPU executing the Software.

(b) The Software can be loaded to the harddrive and the disk kept solely for backup purposes. The Software is protected by United States copyright law. You must reproduce on each copy the copyright notice and any other proprietary legends that were on the original copy supplied by DEARBORN FINANCIAL PUBLISHING, INC.

(c) Configure the Software for your own use by adding or removing fonts, desk accessories, and/or device drivers.

2. **RESTRICTION:** You may not distribute copies of the Software to others or electronically transfer the Software from one computer to another over a network and/or zone. The Software contains trade secrets and to protect them you may not de-compile, reverse engineer, disassemble, cross assemble or otherwise change and/or reduce the Software to any other form. You may not modify, adapt, translate, rent, lease, loan, resell for profit, distribute, network, or create derivative works based upon the Software or any part thereof.

3. **TERMINATION:** This License is effective unless terminated. This License will terminate immediately without notice from DEARBORN FINANCIAL PUBLISHING, INC. if you fail to comply with any provision of this License. Upon termination you must destroy the Software and all copies thereof. You may terminate the License at any time by destroying the Software and all copies thereof.

4. **EXPORT LAW ASSURANCES:** You agree that the Software will not be shipped, transferred or exported into any country prohibited by the United States Export Administration Act and the regulations thereunder nor will be used for any purpose prohibited by the Act.

5. **LIMITED WARRANTY, DISCLAIMER, LIMITATION OF REMEDIES AND DAMAGES:** The information in this software (Materials) is sold with the understanding that the author, publisher, developer and distributor are not engaged in rendering legal, accounting, banking, security or other professional advice. If legal advice, accounting advice, security investment advice, bank or tax advice or other expert professional assistance is required, the services of a competent professional with expertise in that field should be sought. These materials have been developed using ideas from experience and survey information from various research, lectures and publications. The information contained in these materials is believed to be reliable only at the time of publication and it cannot be guaranteed as it is applied to any particular individual or situation. The author, publisher, developer and distributor specifically disclaim any liability, or risk, personal or otherwise, incurred directly or indirectly as a consequence of the use an application of the information contained in these materials or the live lectures that could accompany their distribution. In no event will the author, publisher, developer or distributor be liable to the purchaser for any amount greater that the purchase price of these materials.

DEARBORN FINANCIAL PUBLISHING, INC.'S warranty on the media, including any implied warranty of merchant ability or fitness for a particular purpose, is limited in duration to thirty (30) days from the date of the original retail. If a disk fails to work or if a disk becomes damaged, you may obtain a replacement disk by returning the original disk and a check or money order for $5.00, for each replacement disk, together with a brief explanation note and a dated sales receipt to:

DEARBORN FINANCIAL PUBLISHING, INC.
155 NORTH WACKER DRIVE
CHICAGO, IL 60606-1719

The replacement warranty set forth above is the sole and exclusive remedy against DEARBORN FINANCIAL PUBLISHING, INC. for breach of warrant, express or implied or for any default whatsoever relating to condition of the software. DEARBORN FINANCIAL PUBLISHING, INC. makes no other warranties or representation, either expressed or implied, with respect to this software or documentation, quality, merchantability performance or fitness for a particular purpose as a result. This software is sold with only the limited warranty with respect to diskette replacement as provided above, and you, the Licensee, are assuming all other risks as to its quality and performance. In no event will DEARBORN FINANCIAL PUBLISHING, INC. or its developers, directors, officers, employees, or affiliates be liable for direct , incidental, indirect, special or consequential damages (including damages for loss of business profits, business interruption, loss of business information and the like) resulting from any defect in this software or its documentation or arising out of the use of or inability to use the software or accompanying documentation even if DEARBORN FINANCIAL PUBLISHING, INC. an authorized DEARBORN FINANCIAL PUBLISHING, INC. representative, or a DEARBORN FINANCIAL PUBLISHING, INC. affiliate has been advised of the possibility of such damage.

DEARBORN FINANCIAL PUBLISHING, INC. MAKES NO REPRESENTATION OR WARRANTY REGARDING THE RESULTS OBTAINABLE THROUGH USE OF THE SOFTWARE.

No oral or written information or advice given by DEARBORN FINANCIAL PUBLISHING, INC. its dealers, distributors, agents, affiliates, developers, officers, directors, or employees shall create a warranty or in any way increase the scope of this warranty.

Some states do not allow the exclusion or limitation of implied warranties or liabilities for incidental or consequential, damages, so the above limitation or exclusion may not apply to you. This warranty gives you specific legal rights, and you may also have other rights which vary from state to state.

COPYRIGHT NOTICE: This software and accompanying manual are copyrighted with all rights reserved by DEARBORN FINANCIAL PUBLISHING, INC. Under United States copyright laws. the software and its accompanying documentation may not be copied in whole or in part except in normal use of the software or the reproduction of a backup copy for archival purpose only. Any other copying, selling or otherwise distributing this software or manual is hereby expressly forbidden.

SIGNATURE_____
SIGN IF BEING RETURNED UNOPENED FOR REFUND

SOFTWARE REGISTRATION

Congratulations on the purchase of your new **Corporate Forms Kit** book/disk package. Please complete this form, tear it out, fold, tape and mail it back to us so our software support department will know who you are, should you need to call in for help.

Name _____

Title _____

Company _____

Address _____

City _____ State _____

Zip Code _____

Day Telephone (   ) _____

Fax (   ) _____

Please rate the following products on how useful you would find them in running your business:

1. A small business legal guide that helps you understand legal issues, describes how to protect your assets and provides ready-to-use forms.

    O Not at all useful   O Somewhat useful   O Very useful

2. A collection of business agreements, forms, memos and letters to help you seal the deal in writing.

    O Not at all useful   O Somewhat useful   O Very useful

3. A hands-on guide for showing you how and why to write a business plan.

    O Not at all useful   O Somewhat useful   O Very useful

4. What type of computer do you own?

    O IBM or IBM-Compatible   O 3½" disk   O 5¼" disk
    O Macintosh   O Other

5. Does your computer have a CD-ROM drive?

    O Yes   O No

6. Please tell us about the biggest challenges you face in operating your business.

_____

_____

_____

_____

UPSTART

The Small Business Publishing Company
a division of Dearborn Publishing Group, Inc.
155 North Wacker Drive
Chicago, IL 60606-1719
Software Support: 1-312-836-4400 extension 3400
Hours: Monday – Friday, 9 a.m. – 5 p.m., C.S.T.

IMPORTANT—PLEASE FOLD OVER—PLEASE TAPE BEFORE MAILING

Return Address:

_____

_____

_____

First Class
U.S. Postage
PAID
Dearborn Financial
Publishing, Inc.

BUSINESS REPLY MAIL
FIRST CLASS MAIL PERMIT NO. 88177 CHICAGO, IL

POSTAGE WILL BE PAID BY ADDRESSEE:

UPSTART

Software Registration
155 North Wacker Drive
Chicago, Illinois 60606-9545

IMPORTANT—PLEASE FOLD OVER—PLEASE TAPE BEFORE MAILING

NOTE: This page, when folded over and taped, becomes an
envelope, which has been approved by the United States
Postal Service. It is provided for your convenience.